Leatherhead
1971

SURREY VILLAGES

THE VILLAGE SERIES

Suffolk Villages
Allan Jobson

Surrey Villages
Derek Pitt and Michael Shaw

Yorkshire Villages
Bernard Wood

IN PREPARATION

Cotswold Villages
Devon Villages
Kent Villages

Surrey
Villages

DEREK PITT &
MICHAEL SHAW

Photographs by Richard Rhodes

ROBERT HALE · LONDON

ISBN 0 7091 2339 6

Robert Hale & Company
63 Old Brompton Road
London S.W.7

PRINTED IN GREAT BRITAIN BY
CLARKE, DOBLE & BRENDON LTD.
PLYMOUTH

Contents

Illustrations

Preface

BOTH of the authors of this book have lived and worked in Surrey for well over twenty years and both would have claimed, a year ago, that they knew the county tolerably well. Their experience in writing this book, however, has been a revelation to them, not only in the number and attraction of the villages which form its subject, but also in the remarkable beauty of the countryside, a beauty by no means confined to the well-known and obvious places like Newlands Corner or Ranmore Common.

The Surrey countryside has been, therefore, the real inspiration behind the book; but the authors wish also to express their debt to the very large number of residents in Surrey who have lent them books, told them anecdotes or given them information and, above all, have admitted them to their historic houses where they have been allowed to go everywhere with note-books and camera and have then been regaled with tea and sympathy. This book is an attempt, albeit feeble, to show their gratitude to all these people; also to their professional colleagues who have suffered much from their boring conversation and to their mothers and wives who have seen many days admirably suited for picnics and outings 'wasted' on 'villaging'.

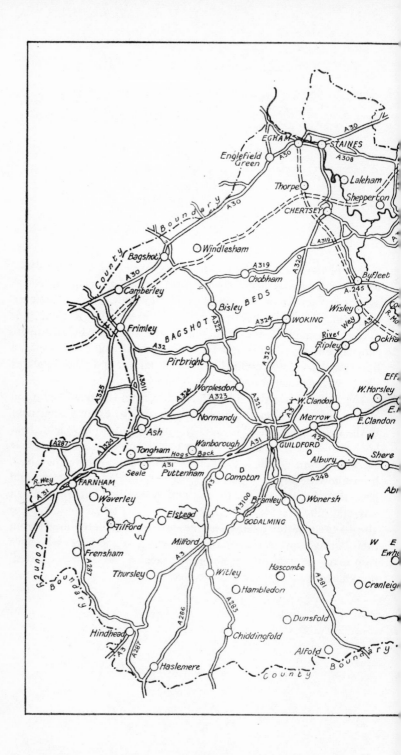

Surrey Villages

I

The Roots

RESEARCH into the age of the earth, by measurement of radio-activity, now, as well as by more traditional methods, yields figures of quite staggering size. The National Debt or even that annual gambling counter, the Budget, employ figures that are entirely outside the scope of our comprehension. So do the geologists. The oldest rocks in the British Isles, the Cambrian, were, they tell us, formed more than 500 *million* years ago.

We do not have to stretch our powers of comprehension to quite this extent in our own survey.

In geological times, the South-east of England was more often under water than not. Even during periods when the waters receded temporarily this part of England was left as a steaming swampland, more often under the sea than not, and it finally appeared as dry land first as a sort of cigar-shaped island, and only gradually assumed its present shape.

By the time we have reached now in our survey, most of the basic constituents of our soil had been formed. The core is clay. The Weald clay grew out of the swamp years. Above this, here and there, comes a layer of Lower Greensand, which ranges in quality from a clayey, loamy sand, more or less fertile, to the porous sandstone, mostly sterile, of Leith Hill and Hindhead where only sparse heathlands are found.

Above that, and a little more recent therefore, is a stretch of another clay soil called Gault. Above that again is the Upper Greensand layer, the greenish-grey sandy subsoil found under the chalk

Downs above Reigate and Betchworth. A formidable crust of chalk covers the Gault and Upper Greensand.

As chalk covers the North Downs now, it probably, at one time, covered the whole of the county. Some relics of an inland sea can still be found on, and in, the chalk, not only in fossilized marine life, not only in the clay-with-flints that covers much of the less steep lower slopes, but in one or two areas of sea-formed sand, such as that at Headley Heath and, maybe, Netley Heath, both of which are now just above the 600-feet mark.

During the time the bulk of the Weald stuck out as an island from the sea, weather and rain worked upon it. The rivers were formed and ran north and south from the main ridge, laying bare the heavy body of clay. The land rose here and sank there, and the thrust that, further south, squeezed the Alpine chain upwards, drove new ridges into the scene.

While this was going on the Thames valley was deepening and a wide area of swampland was draining out into the Rhine, which still ran through a land mass where the North Sea now is. That swampland left behind, above the previous deposits, that other gardener's nightmare, the London clay that stretches, just to the north of the Downs, in a widening wedge from Guildford to London itself.

This is nearly the end of the story. The youngest layers are those of the sandy, gravelly areas of the north-west of the county. The river's action here was to carry down a mass of churned-up rubble and stone and to spread them over a wide region. These gravels are known as Bagshot and Claygate Beds, and they are responsible for the unproductive heathlands of that part of the county.

In this way, then, was the structure of the district formed. As the land became cleared of the overlying water, vegetation began. First, it seems, birch- and pine-woods, with shrubs like juniper and willow. Then the first human inhabitants arrived from the Continent, across the land bridge that still joined England with Northern France and the Netherlands. These were Paleolithic, and later Mesolithic, men, hunters who used rough flint weapons. Then came the glacial periods, three major times of intense cold, the first about 18,000 B.C. and the last between about 8,600 and 8,300 B.C.

During these the vegetation growth virtually died out and the human occupation ceased.

Some time between 7,500 and 5,500 B.C. the average temperature rose and the land slowly sank until, towards the latter of those dates, the last land-links with the Continent were submerged. The North Sea was formed and the strait of Dover was inundated, and the Atlantic could flow through. The shape of England was cut into something near to its present form. With the Atlantic flow the climate became moister, more temperate. Elm and oak invaded the island and became established as the dominant tree cover. The vast forest of the Weald came into being, a forest that was to last, and check southward movement, until the late Middle Ages.

Neolithic man, our first farming stock, now settled in the drier parts, mainly on the chalk uplands, and kept sheep and grew some cereals. They still used flint implements, and there is evidence that they used fire and cut down trees for charcoal. Then the climate became drier. Water supplies became scarcer on the porous chalk, and the settlements came down into the valleys and the plains under the chalk escarpments.

Some time soon after 2,000 B.C. the use of metals was introduced, and the 'Bronze' Age began. Population increased and some penetration and clearance of the forest came about.

New invasions occurred periodically from about 500 B.C. onwards, those of the 'Iron' men. They must have come by boat and they probably approached by way of the Thames. The last of these 'Iron' Age invaders arrived only some fifty years before Julius Caesar. They came from the region of the Marne, small, dark men. These were Celts. Whatever their descendants may pretend, they were not the original inhabitants, but only the last of a succession of pre-Roman invaders. Like other invaders, they mixed with the existing stock and together they formed the British who fought against Rome and then merged with the conquerors to fight against the onslaught still to come.

Pre-Roman man has left, in Surrey, little enough evidence of his existence, and modern farming and housing have wiped away much that once must have been available. Relics of ancient pit dwellings, hollows now with marks of a hearth and of posts to support a roof, have been found near Croydon, Farnham and Abinger. These may represent their owners' last desperate attempts to cope with the freezing temperatures of the glacial ages. Then there used to be a long barrow, a communal Neolithic grave, also near Farnham, but that has been swept to oblivion.

Bronze Age burial mounds, or round barrows, small mounds in which individuals were buried in a crouched position, have been located at Crooksbury Common, Chobham, at Banstead, Frensham, Horsell, Reigate Heath and at Wotton.

The best observable relics of Iron Age occupation are the earthworks, large hill fortresses of which much can still be seen at Anstiebury, near Coldharbour, south of Dorking; at Holmbury Hill, above Holmbury St. Mary, and at Hascombe. These three are all in the Greensand belt. Others, now wholly or partly destroyed, were sited on St. George's Hill, Weybridge, almost obliterated by a housing project, and at Oatlands Park, quite nearby, but that was levelled in the reign of George II by the seventh Earl of Lincoln. An earthwork on Wimbledon Common was levelled in the last century, and vestiges exist on White Hill, near Caterham. The most recently discovered and excavated earthwork is, unusually enough, to be found in the Weald, though not on the Weald clay. This is on Dry Hill, almost in the south-eastern corner of the county.

These earthworks were all probably purely defensive areas into which the local population, under threat of attack, would retire. Several of them are found not far from that ancient track that ran from east to west along the edge of the chalk via the Hog's Back and the southern uplands of the North Downs into Kent.

Several smaller earthworks are to be found in the county, but these are probably later in date and may have been little more than animals' corrals against cold weather or marauders in Romano-British times.

The Roman conquest of the south-east was a speedy business and was finished, once started, in a very few days. The Emperor Claudius came to Britain to witness the action and General Aulus Plautius successfully obliged; he won an overwhelming victory over Caractacus and the South-east accepted terms. Claudius stayed only sixteen days in the country, and by the time he left all was quiet. The German Blitzkreig in Europe was scarcely more efficient.

In the wake of the soldiers and administrators, as in all history, came not missionaries—missionaries are a more modern invention—but the merchants. Like their modern counterparts, they seem to have felt the lure of the Surrey hills, and they set up villas, farms and small industries in the county. Perhaps it is unfair to speculate whether, in Roman times as well, farming was, on occasion, a means of establishing a loss for the benefit of the tax-gatherer.

Roads, the Romans' ultimate deterrent, were laid. The earliest was the Calleva Atrebatum that ran between London and Silchester, and which crossed the north-west corner of Surrey, to cross the Thames at Staines.

Stane Street was constructed to link London with Chichester (Regnum), then an important harbour and regional capital. Finds made along it date from the first and second centuries A.D., and one authority states categorically that it was in use in A.D. 70.

Stane Street was the first breach of the vast Weald forest, now called Anderida Silva. Some 4 miles of the present A29 through Ockley run dead straight along the old Roman road, which then peters out as a farm entrance as the present road swings sharp to the right. From that point it drew a gentle curve round the edge of the sandstone hills down to Dorking. It crossed the Mole by Burford Bridge and ran up the gentler slope of Mickleham Down, through the grounds of Juniper Hall. Its course over the Down is still clear as the 'Roman Road'. Its track is then lost in the urbanization of Epsom and Ewell. It was 20 to 30 feet wide, a $4\frac{1}{2}$-foot thickness of layers of stone, pebble or flint with fine sand or gravel between the layers, well cambered and running on an embankment, or agger.

A branch of this road led north-west from Rowhook, just in Sussex, up to Farley Heath, clearly a very important centre of Roman life in the district since a great villa and temple existed there.

Another major trunk road ran almost due south from London to Clayton in the South Downs, where was an important iron works. This was another solidly constructed road, some 18 to 20 feet wide. The stretch of highway running from Godstone to Blindleyheath via Tilburstow Hill shows the line of it.

The fourth main artery dates from the second century and linked London with Lewes. It ran close to the Roman villa at Titsey and then across Limpsfield Common and thence to Edenbridge.

It is not known how many Roman villas were sited in Surrey. Some twenty-seven have been recorded, all but six on or near the chalk hills. Others may well have existed, still, conceivably, waiting to be uncovered, while others again have, like some of the earthworks, been destroyed. Those that have been excavated have all been smallish buildings of modest design, just a long corridor from which various rooms opened. Some were almost certainly used for industries, that at Titsey for the fulling (washing and bleaching) of cloth, and that on Ashtead Common for tile-making. Farming, too, was surely a preoccupation of all these villas.

Towards the end of the fourth century A.D., the Roman Empire began to disintegrate. The peoples dominated for so long found it possible and profitable to snap at poorly defended sections of the vast frontiers. Saxon freebooters, for long a thorn in the sides of coastal settlements, began to press ever farther into the hinterland. On the Continent the Vandal hordes, the Visigoths of Alaric, for example, attacked and devastated the lines of communications about the beginning of the fifth century. Britannia, the Romans who had settled and married, their descendants, the Romanized local inhabitants, all were left to fend for themselves and probably to disappear in the terror to come.

The history of the next 500 years is uncertain. What is known is wrapped about with legend and hearsay. Even the written accounts, notably the Anglo-Saxon Chronicle, were compiled long after the events they retail. All available evidence, of every kind, only contrives to give a sketchy picture of an era of chaos, raids, invasions and internecine wars which swept repeatedly over the area.

The first wave of powerful oversea invasion began in A.D. 449, when a small body of Danes was invited by King Vortigern of Kent to help him resist attack from the north. These Jutes came, and so did their friends and relations, and they took over. They plundered and massacred and spread out westwards. Saxon pirates joined in the game. They attacked in Southern England and sailed their shallow-draughted boats up the Thames. There is evidence for an important battle at Sarum in 552 against the Britons led by Arthur, and for a battle in 568 between the Saxons and Ethelbert, King of Kent, at Wibbandune, in which the Saxons defeated the Jutish King. Wibbandune may, as some think, be Wimbledon. It may be Wipley. It may not be in Surrey at all.

The name Suthrige is used now and then at this time to classify the area. This is probably the South Domain (regio) of the Middle Saxons, who gave their name to Middlesex. The great forest of the Weald would almost certainly have severed any possible links with the South Saxons of Sussex.

By the latter half of the eighth century it was part of the kingdom of Wessex. The King of Wessex, Cynewulf, was killed by an ambitious atheling (chieftain or thane) while visiting his lady love at Merton. The killer, we are told, was himself slaughtered the next day by loyalist lords.

Some period of peace was achieved in 832 when Egbert of Wessex defeated all opposition.

All too soon, however, that peace was violently shattered by the Vikings, who made, after years of coastal raiding, a major invasion of Kent in 851. They quickly advanced through Kent to London and thence into Surrey. There they were defeated in a great battle at Aclea by the Wessex forces under Ethelwulf. Aclea may be, as tradition has it, Ockley. It is, however, a tradition unsupported by any real evidence, although the proximity of the hill forts of Anstiebury and Holmbury, quite likely still in use then, makes the suggestion an attractive one. Another legend, mentioned by Aubrey, runs that the women of Gatton, above Reigate, slew many Danes after a great battle. There is an Oakley near Gatton, as well as a Battlebridge.

The cycles of warfare and massacre and comparative peace succeeded each other. King Alfred brought the Viking leader to the conference table in 878 and persuaded him to be baptized a Christian. The peace was short-lived. Alfred's son again defeated the Danes at Farnham in 893. In 902 there was a battle at 'The Holme' but there seem to be no guesses at the location of that. In 993 and 994 a fleet of ninety-three Viking ships sailed up the Thames to Staines and laid waste a considerable area. Raid followed raid and the land was repeatedly devastated until in 1016 or 1017 Cnut, who is none other than our childhood's wave-defying hero, came to the throne and set about unifying England, a feat which he achieved by a mixture of statesmanship, tact and firmness. On his death, however, his work was all dissipated by the seizure of his throne by an illegitimate son, Harold Harefoot, who took advantage of the absence abroad of the heir, Harthacnut, and then settled the opposition by cunningly doing away with Cnut's second son, Alfred, and massacring his men at Guildford.

The Saxon kingdom tottered along from then until the arrival of William of Normandy in 1066. The country needed desperately the strong government of William.

And yet it was in these 500 or so bitter and confused years that the main lines of Surrey's development were laid down. The Saxon settlements were the basis of the townships and villages of today. Archaeological evidence suggests that they spread first south-west from the London area along the northern edge of the chalk as far at least as Guildford, and then probably along the Greensand line under the south side of the Downs, penetrating also down the Mole gap to Dorking.

Large Saxon cemeteries have been discovered at Mitcham, Hackbridge, Croydon and Beddington, with smaller burial places along the northern line of the chalk, ending with another large ground at Guildown, on the south side of Guildford. This, is it suggested, contained the bodies from Harold Harefoot's disposal of Alfred's challenge to his throne. The assessment of the location of Saxon settlements is further borne out by the discovery of caches of coins, probably buried in evil days towards the end of the ninth century, one near Croydon and the other at Lower Merriden Farm, near Dorking and not far from Anstiebury.

The oldest churches are at Kingston, where for a time the Saxon kings were crowned, and at Stoke d'Abernon. Saxon work is found in several other churches in the region, not only in the areas already marked as settlements, at Fetcham, Bookham, East and West Horsley, at Albury, Wotton and Shere, but also at Thursley, Witley, Hascombe, Wonersh and Compton, all these last six to the south of Guildford in the sandstone and fertile Bargate Beds districts.

Under the Norman yoke, two great landowners acquired vast

estates in Surrey. One of these was Bishop Odo of Bayeux, brother of William the Conqueror; unfortunately for him, he soon quarrelled with the king and was imprisoned. William II, known as Rufus, released Odo, but the latter's penchant for intrigue was not quenched by his experiences and he was eventually exiled. The other Norman magnate in Surrey was Richard de Tonbridge who possessed thirty-eight manors in the county and had castles at Blechingley and at Ockley. He soon had a serious rival in De Warenne whose estates were at Shere and Fetcham and who also had castles at Reigate and Dorking.

Domesday Book tells us of some of the place-names then in use in Surrey: Chingestune, Fingeham, Wochinges, Godelminge, and from it we learn of the importance in the county, not only of arable farming but also of swine-raising, particularly in the Weald forest. The popularity of hawking is illustrated by the revealing fact that a hawk was worth £6, which was more than the rent-roll for the whole of Weybridge!

The De Warennes became the dominant Surrey family in the twelfth century, but the Clares, descended from de Tonbridge, gained the upper hand when they joined Simon de Montfort in 1263. Simon, the baronial leader against the feeble Henry III, marched through Surrey in that year. The De Warennes suffered a temporary eclipse during these troubled years, when Farnham Castle became the headquarters of organized brigandage.

The rivalry between the two main families was resumed later in the thirteenth century and did not really cease until the Wars of the Roses; it is not true that those fifteenth-century civil conflicts destroyed the power of all the English barons, but it appears to have had a marked effect upon the Clares and the De Warennes, and from this time there were no major aristocrats wielding great power in the county.

The barrier of the Weald meant that roads ran east and west rather than north and south through the county; thus no army passed through from north or from south after Simon de Montfort did so and no ruler made a progress through the county from north to south or vice versa between Edward I (1272–1307) and Elizabeth I (1558–1603). This does not mean that kings did not visit the county at all; on the contrary, the hunting rights enjoyed by them were very considerable. The boundaries of the royal forests survive in a document of 1327 and include the following fascinating areas: Glorney by Glambrugge to Lillford, and Inggfield to Loderlake-huch, the latter attractive-sounding locality being apparently where the borders of Surrey, Berks and Bucks meet.

The Black Death ravaged the county thoroughly on three occasions in the fourteenth century, in 1349, 1361–2, and 1369. The rolls of vicars or rectors found in many Surrey churches bear witness to the high mortality that this dreadful plague brought in its train. The social upheavals that followed it also affected Surrey and there were serious riots in Chertsey and Guildford in 1381, the year of the Peasants' Revolt. A later rebel leader, Jack Cade, may possibly have married a girl from Tandridge.

The Wars of the Roses did not involve Surrey in any actual fighting, but in 1483 there was a rising against Richard III, part of the widespread upheaval caused by his murder of his nephews, the Princes in the Tower. In support of the Duke of Buckingham against the king was Sir George Browne of Betchworth, who was executed in Kent when Richard overcame his opponents. Fourteen years later, the Cornishmen in arms against Richard III's supplanter, Henry VII, marched through the county on their way to battle and defeat at Blackheath in Kent.

Henry VII's magnificent son, deciding that he needed a new palace in Surrey, demolished the village of Cuddington to make room for Nonsuch, the building of which he began soon after the death of Jane Seymour, his third wife. This marvellous building, in the style of the French chateaux built by his contemporary Francis I, was demolished in the middle of the seventeenth century.

Tudor times were not as peaceful as some historians have led us to believe and turbulence remained an outstanding characteristic of the English people. Landowners quite often kept sizeable supplies of arms and armour, and Sir Thomas Cawarden of Blechingley had sufficient weapons to arm over 400 men, as well as sixteen large guns! At about the time of Wyatt's Rebellion against Mary Tudor in 1554, Sir Thomas was arrested because of this enormous armoury, but no evil intention could be proved against him and he was released to resume his normal task of providing entertainments for the royal court. In Elizabeth's reign there was trouble over the cutting of timber on common ground by private owners and this particularly applied to Lord Montague, the iron master whose works may have been at Chiddingfold. There was an increasing tendency for powerful men to encroach upon the ancient rights of their villagers over common lands, especially as timber was coming to be in short supply after extensive use of wood for fuel, ship-building and house-building.

Tudor affairs in Surrey were competently managed by the More family whose country seat was at Loseley. Sir Christopher More possessed great influence and power in the county and was a highly trusted servant of the Tudor monarchy which had a happy knack of enlisting the co-operation of local gentry, a knack which their Stuart successors noticeably lacked. But even the Tudors could not always raise from a county the number of troops that they expected: in 1574–5 Surrey was capable of providing 7,896 soldiers for the royal service in wartime, but when the crisis of 1588 arose, only 1,800 were forthcoming. This year of the Armada brought increased renown to Lord Howard of Effingham, who later became Earl of Nottingham and for some years administered the navy in an outstandingly dishonest and inefficient manner.

When Charles I extended Ship Money to inland counties (a move that enhanced his growing unpopularity), Farnham was assessed for £94, Godalming for £90, and Guildford, surprisingly, for only £53. This would seem to show that Guildford, which had risen in importance as the county town as early as the thirteenth century, was by the seventeenth century in decline.

Surrey villages saw surprisingly little fighting in the Civil Wars of the 1640s. The county was parliamentarian in sympathy and a band of seventy-two men raised at Haslemere by Mr. Quennell, owner of the Chiddingfold iron-works, on behalf of the king, was speedily taken, only twenty-two of his men being armed. He continued to supply Charles with guns until forcibly prevented from doing so. In 1642 there was a skirmish near Kingston, while Farnham was garrisoned for Parliament; its governor, Wither, lost it to the royalist Denham but Waller regained it for Parliament very quickly.

After the first Civil War, there was a royalist rising in 1648 with fighting at Reigate and Ewell and a brief skirmish where Surbiton railway station now stands; Sir Francis Villiers was killed in this. A few years later, shortly before the restoration of Charles II, there was another very small-scale royalist insurrection with a skirmish near Leigh.

Numerous changes took place in the incumbencies of village churches during the Interregnum, many parsons who were loyal to the Stuarts losing their livings to Puritan ministers. In 1662 the Rector of Ockley resigned, presumably because he disapproved of the church settlement of Charles II; he seems to have been the only village incumbent to do so at this time.

The reign of Charles II saw a great increase in the importance of Epsom, then still of course only a village. Its medicinal wells attracted many visitors from London including Charles II, Nell Gwynn and Samuel Pepys, whose famous diary records his impressions of the spa. A poorish specimen of Restoration comedy by Thomas Shadwell is called *Epsom Wells*.

During the later part of the seventeenth century the Onslow family began its rise to power and influence in the county and in the state. Sir Richard Onslow became Speaker to the House of Commons in 1708. The eighteenth century is essentially a period in which village life was dominated by the squire and the parson, and in Surrey, as in other counties, large country houses were being built or rebuilt in great numbers throughout the period; very often the church was adjacent to the house and very often the parson and the squire were related, for the advowson of the living might well be in the latter's gift. Esher, Ashtead and Peper Harow provide examples of eighteenth-century houses, built very near to the churches, which are now schools.

The combination of squire and parson usually exercised a benevolent influence upon village life and the eighteenth century is a time of peace in England's internal affairs, though country life was considerably affected by the wholesale enclosures of the mid-century. Enclosure could lead to depopulation of whole villages as at Albury and as Goldsmith's famous poem shows, and it could seriously lower the standard of living of the peasants by depriving them of the rights they and their ancestors had enjoyed for centuries over the common lands. A rapacious landlord could rob his labourers of these rights and so prevent them from grazing a

cow or feeding pigs on the common ground. In the early nineteenth century, trouble broke out in Surrey with serious riots
among the farm labourers at Capel, Dorking, Woking and other
places in 1830. This agitation took the form of attacks upon land-
lords and their property and caused troops to be called out to sup-
press it. Guildford was virtually in the hands of an angry mob
for two or three days.

After these agrarian troubles were dealt with, Surrey villages
were next affected by the coming to the county of the railway.
Large bands of 'navvies' came into the country to carry out the
necessary work of establishing the London and South-Eastern
line which linked London with Kent and Sussex. It is almost
impossible to exaggerate the significance of the railway in the
lives of Englishmen in the mid-nineteenth century. Prior to its
arrival, the majority of villagers, in Surrey as elsewhere, were
born, lived and died in one small place, often with nothing more
than an occasional visit to the nearest market town to break the
monotony of their lives. The railway, with its compulsorily cheap
fares, meant that at last travel was within the scope of all but the
very poorest. Not even the development of the motor car has had
such a decisive effect, though we shall have occasion later in this
book to remark upon the influence that the internal combustion
engine has had upon village life.

In the Great War, Surrey villagers volunteered, or were later
conscripted, into the Forces in large numbers—as the village war
memorials today show only too sadly. By the time of this War,
British agriculture was in none too healthy a state and the farm
labourer was less well paid and housed and fed than his social
counterpart in the towns. Village life was being shaken out of its
ancient pattern—and this process continued steadily in the period
between the wars. It was then that many Surrey villages lost their
identity, as they were swallowed up by the ever-encroaching
environs of London and as their population grew vastly by the
arrival of commuters.

The outbreak of the Second World War in 1939 exposed Surrey,
in view of its proximity to, or part in, London to the peril of air
raids on a scale far greater than in the Great War. Certainly, when
the Germans overran France and threatened to invade England,

Surrey was deeply involved: the German invasion plan aimed to bring their troops well into the county as their first objective; the line they hoped to reach ran from Southampton to Gravesend via Reigate and in attaining their second-phase objective, north of London, they would have stormed through much of the county. Hence the large numbers of pill-boxes and other defensive works still to be seen in the most unexpected places in Surrey's country districts. Never, mercifully, called upon to fulfil their original purpose they have perhaps been of use in the service of Venus rather than of Mars. Certainly to the historian there is a certain fascination in coming across the remains of an impressive-looking tank trap within a few hundred yards of the ruins of Waverley Abbey!

2

The North-western Plain

S O M E 20 million years ago, the Thames brought down masses of sand and gravel and deposited them in a wide area that now forms the north-west of the county. Most of this region is now relatively infertile, and so great stretches of sandy heathland spread over this corner. These, known to geologists as the Bagshot Beds, were considered so valueless that the army had no difficulty in seizing great tracts for training grounds.

In the Middle Ages the whole region was part of Windsor Great Park, the vast hunting area reserved for the King's pleasure and subject to his special laws. This royal preserve gradually dwindled to the present Park. As Bagshot Heath became free of royal control it fell into the unofficial rule of the highwaymen, whose activities there have found their way into many seventeenth- and eighteenth-century plays, notably into *The Beggar's Opera*, and it is clear that travellers crossing that wide area went in fear of their lives. Apart from that danger, too, there was also the discomfort of the dust thrown up by horses and carriages, which made Defoe liken the place to Arabia Deserta.

It was only where the rivers created a fertile alluvial soil that the early settlements grew up and, for many centuries, the rest of the countryside must have been almost completely uninhabited.

Along the Thames, of course, came the major settlements, Walton, Weybridge, Chertsey and Egham, all now towns. The Abbey of Chertsey plays an important role in the history of several villages. Just across the river from Chertsey there is now, since 1965, a small enclave of Surrey that was carved by the planners out of Middlesex. It contains those two lovely riverside villages of Shepperton and Laleham which have miraculously preserved so much of their eighteenth-century graciousness amid the encroaching suburbia.

Shepperton has an ancient history. In 959, it is recorded, St. Dunstan presented to the Monastery of Westminster 'the possession of Scepertune', whose name suggests that it was a place for keeping sheep. The early church was destroyed by floods at the beginning of the seventeenth century and the present building was erected, probably further from the river-bank, in 1614, with the tower added in Queen Anne's reign. The place is lovingly maintained and, even with the early Victorian box-pews, it has something of the spaciousness of the eighteenth century.

The little square outside the church is quite superb still. Although some of the cottages are earlier, probably, than the eighteenth century, they have been fitted with Adam-style doorways, and the total effect again, with the Anchor Hotel, the 'King's Head', and the fine Queen Anne façade of the rectory, is happily eighteenth century, in spite of a horrid sign that reads "Good Food till Midnight", and a vast garage on the opposite side of the main road.

The hinterland of Shepperton and its green is a dismal procession of hugger-mugger housing, but the riverside is magnificently preserved, and the area round Shepperton Lock, down Ferry Lane, is beautiful without quite becoming chi-chi.

The road along the river-bank from Chertsey Bridge towards Laleham is less precious still and the haunt of the ordinary folk to whom Toni's ice-cream van appeals. Laleham Abbey may have ceased to exist from 1541 onwards, but its lands are still, in parts, a pleasaunce for the populace.

Laleham was originally, it seems, a place of withies or willows, and its good river meadows were quickly annexed for church use, being granted by Edward the Confessor to the Abbey of Westminster, which thus obtained control of almost the whole of this district. The monks who were detached from headquarters to this abbey were often in conflict with their brethren of Chertsey and from them obtained possession of the meadowland across the river called then Mixtenham and the Isle of Burgh, which now appear as Mixnams and Laleham Burway. Apart from this they did build a church.

This is a remarkable little building, late Norman for the most part and built almost wholly and unusually in brick. Inside the arches and the great pillars were encased in stone and plaster, and though some of this has fallen away it is possible to see what the original structure must have been like. The chancel, however, is cluttered up with eighteenth- and nineteenth-century monuments, and there is a modern wooden screen on the north side.

There is a hatchment hanging on the north wall of the aisle, and another, it would seem, raised in the plaster of the south wall. Over the south doorway is an ancient projecting keystone of unusual design, possibly a part of the original building. The west window is modern (1925) and a fine powerful arrangement of people of all colours and nationalities made by W. M. Geddes as a memorial to a former organist.

In the churchyard are buried the third Earl of Lucan, one of the victors (or villains!) of the Crimea, and Matthew Arnold and his wife, and their sons and grandsons. Thomas Arnold settled in Laleham in 1819 and set up a tutorial establishment here before going off with all his large family to Rugby. His brother-in-law, the Reverend John Buckland, at the same time established a preparatory school in Laleham, a school whose harsh discipline appealed, apparently, to the gentlemen of London, for the school continued to flourish for many years. Matthew Arnold often came here to visit the Bucklands and so it came about that the family was buried in this churchyard.

The church is set on a sharp bend of the road among a number of fine houses, some splendidly Victorian but some earlier, notably the eighteenth-century Church Farm and the Queen Anne Dial House. The scene, here again, is spoiled somewhat by the incursion of a garage almost next door to the church itself, whose mechanic was unable, perhaps not unexpectedly, to tell us how to find the vicarage.

Across the river, not far from its patron, Chertsey Abbey, lay, and lies, the village of Thorpe.

It is certainly no new thing for the village of Thorpe—and 'village' is precisely what Thorpe means—to provide a residence for wealthy burghers of London. Probably it was the proximity of the Thames and the convenience of water-borne transportation that led, for instance, William Denham, citizen and goldsmith of the City of London, to settle here in the sixteenth century. He and his wife must have found it salubrious; their tomb is here and their memorial brass in the church shows that they bore five sons and ten daughters. Another who lived here, somewhat later, in the late eighteenth century and into the nineteenth, was Captain Hardy, famous as Nelson's friend. The village is still within easy daily reach of the City, and so it still has a large commuter population. Probably few of them are likely to leave their memorial in the church or to have so large a brood as William Denham.

Whichever way you approach Thorpe, you are likely to see some attractive old houses, cottages smartened up and replete with cocktail bars, farmsteads housing Moguls, mansions made into hotels. Out by Egham is the splendid Elizabethan mansion of Great Fosters, fine Tudor red brick and the royal coat of arms over the door, with the initials E.R. and the date 1578. In the next century, described in his will as "my house of forsters", it was left by Sir John Dodderidge to his son. This magnificent house is now a hotel.

On the road from Chertsey was once the ancient water-mill of Thorpe, a small barn-like building obviously a pitiful remnant of what must have been—what mill wasn't?—a proud and profitable structure. The old mill has now disappeared. If you turn off the Chertsey-Staines highway up to Thorpe by way of Eastley End, so called because it is to the east of the village, you will pass Eastley End Cottage, a comparatively large seventeenth-century farmhouse with some earlier parts still. Lastly, if you happen to come up through Lyne, you will see, away up its drive, Lyne Place, built probably somewhere in the nineteenth century, with classical portico and grey stone façade, and now desolate in the builder's hands. A little nearer to Thorpe is a splendid brick and timber farmhouse with overhanging upper floor. This is Redlands Farm. Even the road is somehow primitive, a farm track only superficially covered with tarmac, it seems, and maintained, for we saw it, by a real, old-fashioned road gang, a survival, surely, of a vanished age, as is Redlands Farm itself.

The Manor of Thorpe was granted before 675 by Frithwald to the Abbey of Chertsey. Under Edward the Confessor it had been valued at ten hides, and at Domesday at seven hides. In hard cash both these estimates had been assessed at £12. *O tempora, o mores!* In 1537, of course, the manor was claimed by the King and then it passed, as with so many of these manors, from family to family. The other main manor house, that of Hall Place, was pulled down in the early nineteenth century, when the present Thorpe Place was built on its site. Even when the abbey held the manor some lands were still in the king's gift, and it is recorded that in 1377 lands named Redwynde were granted for life to John the Parker for keeping the king's deer. The connection with the abbey is preserved in the form of a footpath, raised above the surrounding marshy land in places, that links Thorpe with Chertsey still.

Round the church is a picturesque group of old houses and cottages, ranging in date through from the sixteenth and eighteenth centuries until the present day. On the other side of the road is a well-preserved late seventeenth-, early eighteenth-century example of country-style house. It is called Renalds Herne, by which name the Hall had been known until its rebuilding. Nearby is Blackhouse Farm and its cottages, all of the eighteenth century, and a little further east is the Anglo-Catholic community of Spelthorne St. Mary, in whose outbuildings is a stable block of the sixteenth century and an almost ageless thatched cottage which cannot be less than 300 or 400 years old. Several other splendid old buildings will be found; or an old wall of exact date—1613—by Thorpe Place Cottage; even the village shop, which used to be the school.

The church, towards the beginning of the century, was greatly involved in antagonisms brought about by feuding extremes of churchmanship, and we read that the village constable, in his full regalia, had to attend Sunday services to enable the priest, in his, to celebrate Mass.

The church is not unattractive in spite of the usual sequence of restorations. All that remains of a late Norman building is the doubled chancel arch, unadorned, somewhat roughly formed and the arch a little flattened. The nave itself is probably of the same date, but the addition of two aisles and transepts some time in the thirteenth century left no outward sign of the original nave. The chancel was rebuilt towards the middle of the fourteenth century. The double-basined piscina was put in then, as were the paired sedilia, all these with the ogee-shaped heads. The shelf, or aumbry, to the west of the sedilia, is a later copy of the piscina's shape. The windows at each side of the chancel are also of the same date and have some rather attractive flowing tracery in them.

On the south wall of the chancel is the brass, already mentioned, to William Denham and his wife. He kneels on the left with his five sons behind him, while she kneels facing him, with her ten daughters behind her. The brass is dated 1583. On the floor, under a carpet, is a slightly earlier memorial, a brass, dated 1578, to John Bonde and his wife. He is obviously a wealthy merchant and is wearing a fine fur-edged robe. Here are seven sons and seven daughters, and the family coat of arms is set at each corner of the slab.

An unusual feature of this church is to be seen in the two twin lights or squints that open from the nave into the chancel, one pair on each side of the arch. These are thought to be fifteenth-century work, but they are certainly rather crude openings with heavy cinquefoiled heads, conceivably done by the village mason unused to fabricating delicate stone-work. Their purpose is not quite clear; they may have been intended to allow more light for altars set up in the nave.

The chapel in the south aisle has a piscina also of the fourteenth century and now just outside the chancel arch on that side there hangs a fine silver ikon. Above the chancel arch now is a modern wall-painting which hardly enhances the beauty of the place; it agrees less well with the medieval structure than does the battle-mented, red-brick, seventeenth-century tower outside.

To the west of Thorpe opens out what might be called the millionaire and memorial region. Apart from the old township of Egham, which probably grew up more as a coaching centre than for any other reason, the development is mainly recent, although some old cottages at Englefield Green still officially preserve the right of grazing on the green.

The Norman doorway and Tudor porch at Pyrford Church

Newark Abbey from Pyrford churchyard

Quality Street, Merstham

Horsley Towers

Brasses in Surrey churches: *(left)* Robert Shiers at Bookham, *(right)* East Horsley Church

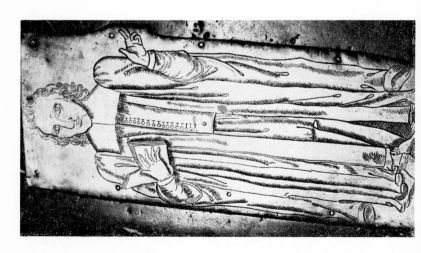

District boundaries are too scientific in this memorial region, the corner where so many monuments are clustered together, all round Cooper's Hill. Englefield Green stands on the higher ground to the south, a pleasant triangle of turf with a few weatherboarded cottages, and, not far away, a spacious cemetery, at the side of which the church looks a little like a cemetery chapel. Yet it was built as a church in 1859, by E. B. Lamb. The pre-Raphaelite movement evidently had its influence, and the Gothic revival is mingled with the new scientific building techniques. As a building it has a stab at everything. Outside it looks modest but inside no stylistic conceit is lacking; brickwork arranged in various decorative manners is mixed with rustic stonework, gaudy glass is set off by Burne-Jones beauties round the Pulpit and by encaustic tiles on the floor. The Collins Guide refers to "eccentric details; lined with strange mixture of stone and brick". This succinct summary is adequate!

On the shoulder of Cooper's Hill, overlooking the Thames and a wide terrain beyond, is the R.A.F. memorial, an austere, white tower with curving wings, on the walls of which all the members of the Commonwealth Air Forces killed in the last war are listed. This is a touching place even though the total effect of the architecture is just a little reminiscent of Hitler's Nuremburg rallying-place. Flowers stand on the sills below and beside the tall lists of names, and in the centre, under the tower, looking out over the vast view, is a small, entirely undenominational praying place, simple and affecting.

Down below this and more easily approached from Staines are the meadows of Runnymede where the Barons bullied King John into signing Magna Carta from which stem many of our cherished liberties. In a way this was little different from the moves of our present-day trades unions to obtain good terms for their members from the employers. Another modest monument not far off celebrates that modern American President who, in his own way and in another hemisphere, attempted to bring freedom to humanity, John F. Kennedy.

Quite a different kind of monument to quite a different kind of man stands up on the hills very close to the county border here. This is to that Duke of Cumberland who was the victor of the Battle of Culloden. He it was who caused Virginia Water to be

C

created, and here, in the Savill Gardens, a good stretch of sandy woodland, is an obelisk to the Duke. It overlooks a smaller expanse of water, now called the Obelisk Pond, and a fair number of people come here to wander through the trees and by the water. They come, however, subjected to a frightening barrage of legal phraseology: "No visitor shall handle, destroy, cut, or injure any shrub, leaf, plant, flower, fruit or seed, or pick or take away or have in their possession after being so picked or taken away, any bough, leaf, plant, flower, fruit or seed." So there!

It is round the boundaries of Virginia Water that the wealthy have settled in greater profusion. The lake itself was constructed by Paul Sandby, the water-colourist. All round this countryside, among the fir trees of the healthy sandy uplands, attached by social navel-strings to Wentworth Golf Club, are dotted the estates and the stylistic exuberances of the nineteenth- and twentieth-century tycoons.

Southward from this land dedicated to Mammon comes the region dedicated to Mars, where the highwaymen gave place to the brutal and licentious soldiery. It is a very large area and there are constant reminders: "DANGER—KEEP OUT—MISSILE RANGES—HIGH EXPLOSIVES", and so on, written on notices that line the roads and seal off some beautiful countryside.

Much of the district was once a part of Chobham and its name appears in Chobham Common and Chobham Ridges, which are some 6 or 7 miles away from the village. This is explained, of course, by the fact that the country was, at one time, so entirely unpopulated. There were hamlets along the line of the Hale Bourne, and at Bisley, but considerable tracts were too infertile to support settlement and so Chobham extended over a wide area. Chobham now is on the eastern edge of armydom.

In 1853 the British Army paraded 8,000 troops on Chobham Common to be reviewed by Queen Victoria—an unprecedented event which was duly commemorated by a small obelisk. The Victorian army was quite unaccustomed to being royally inspected *en masse* and as yet there was no thought of anything as horribly Prussian and professional as manœuvres, but the review on Chobham Common was, in fact, the forerunner of Aldershot, for the temporary camp set up to house the troops in 1853 was translated into the permanent barracks and parade squares of Aldershot within a few years. In much more recent times, the common has been used as a tank training ground; what would Victoria and her red-clad soldiers have thought of these clanking monsters? The pre-Crimean army is not the only ghost that can be aroused on the common for on its west side are three Saxon barrows.

The monks of Chertsey made a great pond on this common and called it Gracher's Pond or Gratuis Pond or Gratious Pond; Aubrey spelt it Gracious Pond, but 100 years after his time it was described as choked with weeds and its site was eventually occupied by the farm which bears its name. Cobbett found this fine stretch of heath poor and unproductive and was seemingly blind to its beauty, enhanced as it is by the groups of pine trees which break up the stretches of gorse and heather. Chobham itself was probably Ceabba's settlement in Saxon times and there were Roman coins found in some profusion suggesting a sizeable camp on the old Saxon site. Later Chobham came under the sway of the Abbots of Chertsey.

In 1254 Geoffrey de Bagshot held Chobham from the abbot who was paid, *inter alia*, 10s. 4d., twelve gallons of honey, two sheep, two quarters of oats, one ploughshare and the loan of a horse twice a year to take one of the Chertsey monks to Winchester. In the thirteenth century also, the people of the village obtained the right to bury their dead in the churchyard instead of having to take them to Chertsey Abbey; they had to pay 20s. and 10 pounds of wax annually for this privilege, for the medieval church was fully aware of the financial advantages to be obtained from carrying out its duties.

There is today one grand reminder of the great days of Chertsey Abbey, for the church porch is believed to have come from the abbey when it was dissolved by Henry VIII in 1538. It would be pleasant to think that this belief is fully justified, for the porch is a fine one and it is entirely fitting that at least one church in this area should retain a permanent memorial of the abbey which for so long dominated the district.

Restoration has hit St. Lawrence Church hard, but much of interest remains. There is a massive chest with three locks which would seem to date from the middle of the thirteenth century, the great roof-beams are original, the font of wood is Tudor; best of all are the traces of Norman work in the arcade which was created by the piercing of the old wall to give access to a Lady Chapel which was added in about 1160. This Lady Chapel today possesses an ancient piscina which was found when the chancel of the main church was rebuilt in 1898, and is also notable for the extraordinary roof-beams.

In the chancel is a memorial to Nicolas Heath, Archbishop of York in the reign of Mary Tudor, who died in the Tower in 1578 since he adamantly refused to conform to the Anglican settlement of Mary's successor and half-sister Elizabeth. Mr. Ogilvy says that Heath retained Elizabeth's favour despite his obduracy and that she often visited him in his Chobham home, though this hardly squares with the fact recorded on his memorial tablet that he died a prisoner in the Tower. Chobham in the later part of the sixteenth century had as vicar Thomas Taunton, who held the living from 1595 until 1652 in which year he died at the respectable age of 117! There are some fascinating clergymen associated with this church as well as the Methuselah-like Taunton: the first vicar, appointed in 1324, rejoiced in the name of William de Dagelyng-gesworth; in 1800 the Reverend Richard Cecil, on becoming vicar, reported that the parish was "sunk in the depths of ignorance and immorality"—by no means an unusual state for rural parishes at this time when the Church of England had barely been aroused from its sloth by the challenge of Wesley.

St. Lawrence occupies a suitably dominant position in the attractive village; near to it is an old inn, 'The White Hart' (it is noteworthy how often this is the title of public houses in Surrey villages), and on the space between the church and the hostelry there used to be a pig market on Sunday mornings, from which the farmers, we may assume, proceeded to the service having paid their homage to Mammon. Almost opposite the church is a lovely house, almost certainly Tudor, which was a grocer's shop until recently. This has a profusion of beams and of ancient cupboards, while the outbuildings include a large shed in which can still be seen bakers' ovens.

There are many other fine old cottages and houses in Chobham, notably the oddly named Frogpeel House and the delightful Laurel and Canon Cottages. There was once a prominent resident called John de Pentecost whose name appears to have been corrupted into Pennypot, there being a cottage of this name; so there are reminders enough of the long history of Chobham village.

The main road to the west out of Chobham follows the Hale Bourne and the Windle, a line of rich soil that lends itself to the market-gardens that flourish there, as, doubtless, they have for centuries. Near West End is the magnificent seventeenth-century Brook Place that looks, with its fine Dutch gables, much as Abinger Manor must once have looked.

This westerly corner of Surrey presents a curious amalgam of attractive and extensive heathlands and somewhat dull, over-grown villages of which Bagshot and Windlesham are the chief. Indeed, Windlesham claims to be the largest village in the county, a claim which would no doubt be hotly contested by Ling-field.

Windlesham has few distinctive features: its church is on the site of a previous church destroyed by fire in 1676, but any visitor hoping to see a prime example of late seventeenth-century archi-tecture will be disappointed, for the restoration of 1875 was so absolutely complete as to destroy practically every vestige of the Stuart edifice. The seventeenth-century pulpit survives and there is a copy of Bishop Jewel's *Apology* in a case at the side of the chancel-opening, but modern taste will hardly agree with an early nineteenth-century comment "there is much fine work in marble and coloured tiles in the chancel" nor with the same author's commendation of the stained glass. One window—which is not commended!—is the memorial for a major who was killed at the hard and bloody Battle of Inkerman in the Crimean War.

Next to the church is a fine house called 'The Cedars', and there are a few old cottages in the village, which is very large and very straggling; its population today contains a number of very wealthy people who enjoy the excellent communications with London and the rural peace that the neighbourhood offers at weekends.

Bagshot is even more military than Windlesham; the Army Chaplains' Headquarters are here and the Scots firs which are such a feature of the landscape seem to have been planted in some places by someone with a delight in military lines. A vast motorway is at present in construction between Loudwater and Bagshot and will doubtless have the effect of taking away some of the traffic that now pours through the main street despite the existence already of a by-pass. Bagshot church is of late nineteenth-century construction, and attractive buildings in the village are hard to find, though mention must be made of the handsome Queen Anne's House which is now a very pleasant restaurant.

Yet another village in this area of Surrey with unmistakable military connotations is Bisley, the place which most people associate with the sport of shooting at targets. Here annually the King's Cup is contested for, as well as many other major trophies including the Ashburton Shield for public schools. Curiously enough, though the school at which the present authors teach has entered the Ashburton competition for many years, neither of us had ever visited the village until we began work on this book. We were, therefore, surprised to find that Bisley village differed very little from other villages in the county and that its peace was undisturbed during the summer afternoon we spent there by the rattle of fire from the ranges. The church indeed is most delightfully situated at a considerable distance from the firing areas. It is dedicated to St. John the Baptist and its age is attested by its outward-sloping nave walls and by a magnificent timbered porch, unusually at the west end of the church, which dates from the twelfth century, some of whose timbers are original. Some of the names scribbled on the wood have early eighteenth-century dates after them and that this evil custom is by no means dead is proved by some large initials with 1970 after them.

In the restoration of 1873 the west gallery was a casualty, but fortunately sufficient of the old church has survived to make it both interesting and attractive. There is, on the south wall, what is described as a piscina, though our suggestion is that it is in fact a holy water stoup which once flanked an entrance door now blocked up. The pulpit is Jacobean; one of the bells is the second oldest in Surrey, dating from 1310.

The first rector listed on the board in the church began his work in 1283 at which time the church was very much under the aegis of Chertsey Abbey; indeed the inhabitants of Bisley were then, and for many years after, employed in the making of candles for that abbey. A few hundred yards from the south-west corner of the church is a spring which used to provide water for baptisms and which was known as John the Baptist's Well.

The delightful setting of this church, amid fields, enhances its beauty, and the churchyard with its venerable gravestones is perfectly kept. Though it is some distance from the village centre, the inhabitants must count themselves fortunate in the possession of such a lovely building in a village which otherwise lacks character.

Ranges and barracks cover the district. Knaphill is just next door. Not far away are the Pirbright ranges. Only the vast cemetery of Brookwood, established there because of the sandy soil which was fairly infertile and, one supposes, also because the sand made digging easy, provides some relief (if that is the right word!) from the arts of war.

At Pirbright we are still in the heart of the military area, exemplified by notices forbidding W.D. vehicles to use certain roads. Those readers who have served in the armed forces may therefore appreciate that near the village is a common which rejoices in the name Bullswater.

Pirbright's large green is divided, like Caesar's Gaul, into three parts by roads cutting across it. The size can be gauged by the fact that the second largest of the three portions is big enough to provide a good cricket ground. Curiously situated at the end of the green is a school, the architecture of which defies description; it can perhaps be likened to the illegitimate offspring of a barracks and an eastern temple. The village was once the home of the Earl of Essex, Elizabeth I's ill-fated favourite; on the site of his mansion an eighteenth-century house was built which has been much restored; its name is Henley Park. To the south-west of the village is a manor house some of which is sixteenth-century. Part of the extensive common land is Burners Heath, a name which suggests that at one time charcoal-making was a local industry.

There are some good houses round the green, notably the White Hart Inn: though the inside is heavily over-furnished with a profusion of brass ornaments, horseshoes and various knick-knacks, the pub itself is an attractive one from the outside. Near it, and on the same side of the green, is 'The Cricketers', which looks to be late seventeenth century and has a window blocked in to avoid Pitt's window tax of the late eighteenth century.

Off the green towards the church is the brick and timber Mill House and the manor house already mentioned. Ford's Farm and its neighbour Burners Farm are other attractive houses in this pleasant village.

The church is mainly noteworthy because Sir Henry Stanley, the journalist-explorer who found Livingstone, is buried in its churchyard; having lived in Pirbright, he died there in 1904 and a massive block of unhewn granite marks his grave, while there is a memorial plaque to him inside the church. The church itself is a strange building; from the outside it looks much older than it is, for it was rebuilt in 1783 to replace a church presumably burnt down. There is a gallery at the west end which extends along the north side; the east end is late Victorian.

A Bible box dated 1668 and a churchwarden chest also of the seventeenth century are really the only interesting furnishings of a disappointing church whose interior so oddly belies its exterior and which hardly does justice to its setting.

Another very proper military church is, naturally enough, at Frimley, at present a fast-growing place on the edges of Camberley. Up to 1825 this had been but a small chapel served by Ash parish. Census records show why the new church was needed; in 1801 there were 532 inhabitants, in 1811, 702, and in 1821, 1,284, the increase being due, it was assumed, to the "improved neighbourhood of the Military College at Sandhurst".

St. Peter's is a very neat and well-kept church. There is a gallery running round three sides of the nave, presumably for the soldiery, while the officers and the civilians sit below. The churchyard is large and contains the graves of numerous army officers, one artist, and Admiral Sturdee, who in 1925, was buried there under a cross made of timber from the old H.M.S. *Victory*.

Opposite the church is a modern architectural curiosity, a housing estate built in an idiosyncratic semicircular style the rationale of which is difficult to understand. This is only one example of the very considerable development that is going on here. Frimley is a boom town and the old woodlands are being rapidly eaten away by the builders. Fremma's woodland clearing, from which Frimley derives, will soon lack trees altogether, a sad day! Meanwhile it is a bright and lively place, full of energy and bustle, typified by the new church out among the new houses, St. Francis', where the church proper, quite a small and plain one, is joined to the hall where the kids gather with their mothers for play and knitting. It's all unstuffy and young.

Most of Frimley stands on the good river gravels laid there by the Blackwater river, and so does Ash Vale. Ash itself, oddly enough, stands just on the London clay, though its church is on a small pocket of gravel. The old manor and the parish extended for a long way up the river valley and enjoyed, therefore, some reasonable agricultural prosperity.

In the twelfth century, Esche; in the thirteenth century, Assche; in the fourteenth century, Asche; in the sixteenth century, Ashe; today, simply Ash; there is a whole history of the spelling of English place names in these facts—and those who complain about the complexity of English spelling in modern times may care to ponder over the thirteenth-century version of this village's name.

A church at Ash is mentioned in Domesday Book; it had been by then given to Chertsey Abbey but much land in the parish was taken away from the monks and given to laymen late in the thirteenth century. In 1537 the advowson of the church passed into the hands of Henry VIII after the dissolution of Chertsey Abbey, and his son, Edward VI, gave it to Winchester College which still holds it.

The church, dedicated to St. Peter, was originally Norman but today its oldest portions, such as the south door and a lancet in the window of the old chancel, are early thirteenth-century and the tower is over 200 years younger. The south door, which is round-headed, is 1170 and the porch with its wood framing is Tudor.

Two brass tablets on the south wall of the old chancel commemorate Thomas Manory, who died in 1516, and his daughter Anne Vyne; the font is a very handsome example of seventeenth-century wood-carving, the bowl being leadlined. The Parish registers date from 1548 but do not cover the reign of the Roman Catholic Queen Mary nor the period of the Commonwealth. There are some late seventeenth- and early eighteenth-century entries which give us some insight into the life of those periods. Thus in 1694 the village can congratulate itself upon escaping the dire effects of a smallpox epidemic which had ravaged London. In Ash, only four people died that year, three of them from old age and the fourth from being scalded to death in a brewing vessel. There are in St. Peter's two very typical eighteenth-century wall tablets with verse epitaphs:

> No racking pains do now this corpes molest
> Which in its life time had so little rest.
> For now he is dead the gout and stone are fled
> And left him quietly to sleep on his bed.

This is the memorial to Edward Dawe who died in 1718. Anne Newnham is commemorated in a more dramatic vein:

> From earliest youth, sore press'd by varied woes
> In vain this child of Sorrow sought repose;
> Unnumber'd Phantoms hover'd round her gate
> The ruthless ministers of human fate
> Wan disappointment, Pain, and Faded Care,
> Eye-swollen grief and joyless, cold Despair,
> And as the ghastly spectres swept along
> Her eager eye would oft explore the throng,
> Demanding Death, Death only came not near
> His stroke delaying where he saw no fear.

In spite of this the lady died at the age of 78!

Ash has some good cottages, notably one next to the church which used to be the seventeenth-century Hartshorn Inn and which was well restored in 1904. There is the Old Rectory of the sixteenth century with later additions. The Old Manor Cottage and the Old Moat Cottage were formed from the moated manor house. Two pubs, 'The Greyhound' and the 'Bricklayer's Arms', are of the seventeenth and the eighteenth century respectively, the 'Greyhound' having been refaced in 1930. But Ash really is a modern place which has grown immensely with housing estates and the shops needed to supply them.

As Ash and the other villages on this side of the county have become usurped for the military overspill from Aldershot, it is a relief to turn eastward again, though even Normandy, where Cobbett died, has not been immune from development. It is an

uninteresting little place containing little old building. One seventeenth-century cottage there now is but the headquarters of a
caravan site.

The older part of Worplesdon is scattered around an oblong
village green under the sharp little hill that, apparently, gave it its
name. Warple meant a raised pathway, here leading to the dun,
or hill. It was an early settlement and the various commons have
been the scene of prehistoric discoveries, a ditch on Whitmoor
Common, some Bronze Age tumuli, and a Roman villa on Broad
Street Common. The hilly nature of the countryside, which made
it the site of a semaphore on the London-Portsmouth communication system in the eighteenth century, probably made it a useful
centre for primitive defences, and the proximity of the Wey, with
its good alluvial soil, probably interested early farmers. Pockets
of brick earth led to the establishment of brick- and tile-works,
and market gardening has been a prosperous industry here as well.

Worplesdon now is just far enough from the railway to attract
only the wealthiest inhabitants; the mini-mansions of our age lurk
there up private roads and behind close-growing hedges. The church
has the same well-heeled air, an air of distinction that is added to,
doubtless, by its being under the patronage of Eton College. This
patronage has been of practical value to the church, since many
of the fine furnishings have, at various times, been brought there
from the college, a case, perhaps, of the poor relation being kitted
out from the cast-offs of wealthy Uncle Harry.

It is a noble church all the same, well-proportioned and with a
fine square tower. The chancel dates from the thirteenth century
and is slightly offset from the nave, which came in the following
century. The handsome altar rails and the pulpit are seventeenth-
century work and were brought from Eton.

There is good glass in the nave windows. It is all fourteenth-
century work but was, none of it, originally set there. It was
gathered together in 1802 and fitted into the east window. In
1887, however, the present east window was inserted and the old
glass distributed around the nave. In the north wall, in the easternmost window, are two scenes which appear to us to include the
Annunciation, with some beautiful colouring, and in the other
window, with two coats of arms, are the figures of a bishop and

of a kneeling monk. On the south side there are several coats of arms, including the red roses of Jasper, Earl of Pembroke, uncle of Henry VII, and the royal arms of Henry VIII impaling those of Anne Boleyn.

Among the memorial tablets to be found are one to Donald Tovey, the musicologist, and another to the Reverend Thomas Chamberlayne, Fellow of Eton College, dated 1801 and extolling him that he

> rebuked the bold, but bade the timid rise,
> And gave new Strength and Wisdom to the wise.

A very fair summary of the perfect schoolmaster!

All the roads round Worplesdon, in summer, run through the great heaths ablaze with campion and blackberries, under the cool green of silver birches. They stretch out like this almost up to the river itself, where the lush meadows display the difference in the soil. The river flows peaceably here and swans ride on the water easily and proudly. It is over this quietness that Send church looks out.

Send is not really one place at all but a collection of scattered hamlets which end in Holme Heath, or Green. The church is a longish way from the chief centre of population and is most delightfully situated. It is a very fine church indeed, part of which dates from the twelfth century when it was only a Mass chapel for the pilgrims. Only about 1600, after it had been greatly enlarged, did it become the parish church of Send (as the village was then called) and of Ripley. The latter broke away to become a parish in its own right as recently as the end of the last century. Though not a fully-fledged parish church until it had been in existence for some considerable time, Send's list of vicars begins in 1289. Unhappily, a devastating fire caused very serious damage to this church in 1963, in which the Elizabethan gallery was badly damaged and many of the old pews. Fortunately, the work of restoration has been carried out with great skill. A brass in the chancel, to Laurence Slyfield and his wife Alys who lived early in the sixteenth century, survived the fire, as did a good chest which was once used as a safe. A curious feature of the church today is that the pews are placed in such a manner as virtually to block the aisle, making any form of procession in the church an impossibility.

On the left of the church is a handsome house called Send Grove, and on the right there is a fine old farm with extensive outbuildings. With the church itself, these are really the main survivals (together with a few houses on the narrow road which leads down to the church) of old Send.

The church is near the Wey, in a wide stretch of alluvial soil that makes for good agriculture, but much of this enormous parish consists of less productive gravels, and it even extends into the London clay beds, on the very edge of which stands Ripley.

Like Oxted and Blechingley in the east of the county, Ripley is a village which is torn apart and almost destroyed by a main road, the A3. Fortunately, its main street, through which the ceaseless traffic pounds, is broad and lined by willows, but its numerous old buildings must surely be in grave danger of having their foundations shaken by the weight of vehicles passing them. In this High Street there is the brick and timber Anchor Inn, which is Tudor; the Manor House opposite, with Dutch gables, built in 1650; and Cedar House, formerly the George Inn, which is a half-timbered house, partly sixteenth- and partly seventeenth-century. There is also another handsome house, opposite the church, which is Georgian and has a bricked-up window over the porch, and next to the ugly church hall there is a house built in 1597, which is now a dry-cleaner's establishment.

In Rose Lane, south of A3, there are yet more old houses which enable us to realize that this is a village of considerable antiquity. Turner's Cottage, Vintage Cottage (aptly named), Rambler Cottage are outstanding examples in this area.

The village green has for long been the scene of village cricket matches, for the history of the club goes back to the eighteenth century, and the elms surrounding it add considerably to its beauty.

Ripley's church, for so long only a chapelry of Send, was almost completely rebuilt in 1845–6. The chancel alone remains much as it did at the time of its building, about the middle of the twelfth century. The only 'improvement' made here during the rebuilding was in the form of that Victorian ecclesiastical fetish of raising the floor. This has the effect of falsifying all the vertical dimensions.

Round the chancel, below the level of the windows, runs a remarkable string course. This is an elaborate and finely sculptured line of interwoven spiral bands set with diamond-shaped leaves. In the corners are triangular spaces filled with star-shaped leaves. Along the edge is a flowing nail-head surround, and it all constitutes a very beautiful and probably unique work of art.

The east window was inserted about 1230 and consists of three linked lancets. In that wall, by the altar is an aumbry and a piscina with a square bowl, and in the south wall is a credence recess, a shelf for the elements of Mass before their consecration. In the north wall are four recesses believed to be the remains of an Easter Tabernacle, where the Crucifix and the reserved sacrament were placed on Maundy Thursday and taken out again on Easter Day to represent the Resurrection. Most churches had these at one time but they were almost all walled up or destroyed in some time of anti-popery drive.

Just over a mile to the north-west of Ripley stand the dismal remains of Newark Priory, a few gaunt walls mostly propped up here and there by concrete buttresses in the middle of muddy river meadows. It was founded in the middle of the twelfth century and, through many important benefactions and by dint of crafty ecclesiastical skulduggery, the canons became large landowners and powerful, even awe-inspiring, figures in the district, and their holdings stretched to Stanwell, in Middlesex, and Leigh, in mid-Surrey. They were dispossessed in 1539.

Another historical event in this parish concerned the Cornish rebels, marching in 1497 against the authority of Henry VII. They crossed the Wey at a place called St. Thomas' Waterings, which may have been somewhere near Send church. There they had a skirmish with the royal troops, who, indeed, had to fall back and lost contact with the rebels, who pressed on with all speed to Kent, there to be finally defeated. It is possible that the royal troops retired to the heights around Pyrford that overlook the water meadows round Newark Priory. A somewhat imaginative history of Pyrford church in the porch suggests that Thomas Cromwell, in 1539, supervised the bombardment of the priory from the church hill—presumably because the prior and his canons were resisting the dissolution of their house. It can hardly be imagined that Cromwell, upon whom much of the burden of state affairs rested at this time, would have taken an active part in attacking a small priory, even if, which is also improbable, the prior had been so rash as to offer resistance. In fact the Prior of Newark was awarded a small pension by the State, which hardly suggests any resistance to the take-over.

Pyrford church is Norman, complete and virtually unspoilt; even the Tudor porch which leads to the Norman doorway seems in keeping. The door has mouldings of billet and chevron design and the remains of a holy water stoup can be seen on the right. The timbered porch is 9 feet by 5, and it is perhaps a pity that the left-hand inside wall has been used for a series of coloured drawings purporting to give the church's history (including the Thomas Cromwell episode).

There can, however, be no complaints about the interior, with its marvellous timbered roof, particularly the part of it over the rood-beam. The pews are of the fifteenth century, the pulpit Jacobean, there are two consecration crosses in the chancel opposite each other and a third on the west wall.

On the opposite side of the nave is the real pride and joy of this church, a wall-painting fresco of 1140 (the date of the building), over which, some sixty years later, another painting was superimposed; not until the latter was repaired did the older figures beneath come to view. The fresco is a psychomachia, or depiction of a battle between vices and virtues, and there are mounted figures placed on the ground line with a decorative border above instead of below as is usual. At the bottom right is a row of figures whose identity and purpose have apparently baffled experts. At the risk of exciting the latters' scorn we hazard the opinion that the figures, with their staves and conical hats, are pilgrims progressing towards the cathedral which may be the vague shape to their left; if, however, this fresco is contemporaneous with the church then Canterbury is not likely to be their destination, since Becket was not murdered until thirty or so years after the building of this church.

The top painting shows two scenes from the Passion of Christ, on the left the Scourging (the tied hands and feet of Christ can be clearly discerned) and on the right, it is thought, Christ appearing

before the throne of God. The fact that the bearded Christ is turning away from the figure of God is simply because only wicked men
were shown in profile in medieval art.

The chancel arch is a splendid example of Norman masonry; that
the evil practice of name-carving is not a recent one can be proved
by the fact that a certain Henry Slifold scratched his name with
great clearness on the right-hand pillar of this chancel arch—in
1619.

The modern frontal in place when we visited Pyrford is, perhaps more suited to a church of contemporary design, but there
can be no denying the fact that this beautiful twelfth-century
building should be visited by all those who appreciate the genius
of Norman architects and craftsmen.

There was a time when Ockham occupied a more important position than it does now. The parish covers a large area, stretching
beyond the A3 into the fertile regions along the banks of the Wey
that now sustain the R.H.S. Gardens at Wisley. The village lies
back from the main road, to the east, and straggles unharassed
along its byroads, round the outskirts of Ockham Park. It is still,
as it always has been, an agricultural place, lying mostly on good
river gravels, fed by two streams that run into the Wey, and not
too much beset by commuterdom. Council estates have passed
it by, and the roads are scattered with the mellow red brick of
good, solid, pre-nineteenth-century building. What restoration and
reconstruction has been done has been skilfully handled. Bridge End
Cottage, for instance, with the stream still flowing under its wing,
is a lovely building, and so are its neighbours. Perhaps the only
flaw is the pseudo-Gothic block of the Hautbois Inn. The excellence
of its cuisine cannot disguise its architectural effrontery.

The relative freedom from the customary draggle of cheap-jack
bungalows is due to the ownership, for centuries, of the whole
village by the lords of the manor. It was auctioned off only fairly
recently. Now that the safeguards are down, what horror may not
soon be foisted here?

Ockham Manor was clearly an important holding. The Domesday Book records it as held by Richard de Tonbridge. It remained
in the hands of the Clare family for several centuries, and its lords
are woven into and through the history of England, a savage and

View from the belltower of West Clandon Church

Oxted

Godstone

The 'Town Hall' at Gatton

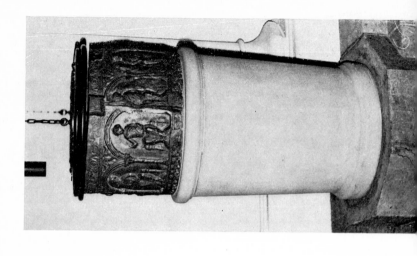

(left) The carved pulpit in Gatton Church. (right) the Norman font in Walton Church

bloody strand in that fabric. Death in battle and death at the executioner's block show not so much the fickleness of the Clares, one of whom was created Duke of Buckingham in 1444, as the waywardness of royal succession. It was not until 1521 that Edward, Duke of Buckingham, was beheaded for treason, an easy enough crime to commit under Henry VIII, and the manor passed out of the family's keeping. By the eighteenth century it was acquired by Peter King, scion of honest burghers of Exeter, who became Lord Chancellor of England and died, in 1734, as Lord King, Baron Ockham. The Italianate house which, in the hands of his successors in the early nineteenth century, replaced the earlier building, is being rebuilt in the authentic manner of earlier days.

The church stands within the confines of the park, some hundred yards from the road along a pot-holed track. It is a handsome building among its tall trees, but, although little touched by the dead hand of the experts, except for the insertion of some sickly glass, it shows scant evidence of the loving hand of the living. There is an air of damp and disinterest, which is a pity, because there is much to appeal to the amateur.

It is a neat nave-and-north-aisle structure, with a strong square tower at the west end. What immediately strikes the visitor is a rare range of seven closely grouped lancets at the east end. These were set there in the middle of the thirteenth century, and the remains of the earlier three-light window can still be seen on the outside. The roof is of mellow brick again, as are the buttresses, and there are tiles set in the fifteenth-century tower. It is tempting to guess that these might be Roman, as at Ashtead, for example, but there is no record of Roman finds in the district.

The original fabric dates probably from the twelfth century, but much was rebuilt about 1220, when the chancel was enlarged and the north aisle added. The tall, narrow, round-headed arch at the west end may be a relic of the primitive edifice. That there was once a rood-loft is made clear by the existence still of parts of the staircase. In the south wall of the chancel are a double piscina and a single seat whose sides go up to the window-sill above it. On the floor on that side of the altar is a good small brass, of a priest in full vestments, showing round the collar the rough swastika which was the early church's transparent disguising of

D

the cross. This is a memorial to Walter Frilende, Rector in about 1350. On the other side of the altar are the brass figures of John and Margaret Weston, dating from 1483 or thereabouts. In the chancel, too, are the stem and base of the thirteenth-century font in Purbeck marble and two fourteenth-century stall-ends that now support a priest's seat.

All this is interesting and could be excitingly displayed by the superb lancets, so neat in their slender, soaring shafts of purbeck marble, which end in finely wrought capitals of designs of leaves. The arched heads are encrusted with sprightly dog-tooth moulding. How magnificent these beautifully proportioned lights would be if they were filled with good plain glass, through which the sky, clouds and trees would fill the place with their glory! The coloured glass that is there is fairly modern and, however much a labour of love, is tawdry in that splendid frame. The encaustic tiling and the sheathing on the walls, as well as empty bases in the squint from the north chapel, and a clutter of odds and ends, not to mention the organ that squats heavily in the chapel, all serve to destroy the inherent nobility of that chancel and its window. You leave it all in a mood of depression and furious frustration at an opportunity so woefully missed, at beauty so wantonly squandered, and it is hard to focus on the other treasures, the remains, in the chapel, of a fifteenth-century niche under which a delightful little head has miraculously been preserved and some genuine woodwork of the same period in the ceiling of the aisle and at the eastern end of the nave. This ceiling-work of a dark and light diamond pattern with great ornate bosses at the intersection is almost unique and is crying out for a craftsman's skilled attention.

Not even the florid self-satisfaction of the eighteenth-century King mausoleum tacked on to the north wall can contrive to bring you out of your frustration at the wastage.

Lord Chancellor King was probably not the finest intellectual flower of the village. It seems almost certain that William of Ockham, one of the giant intellects of the fourteenth century, who challenged two popes and charged them with error and heresy and who came through unscathed, was born here. It is possible, though without such strength of evidence, that two other notable theologians of that age, John Occam and Nicholas Occam, may also have been natives of this parish. While the lords were battling and losing their heads in clashes with the temporal ruler, it seems that the thinkers may have been similarly in opposition to the spiritual King. Ockham, it appears, can lay claim to be the breeding-ground of staunch and obstinate men.

Wisley Gardens, the Royal Horticultural Society's glorious display centre and testing ground, are really in Ockham, just beside Ockham Mill. The grounds stretch over some 200 acres of land ranging from heathlands on the Bagshot Beds to the rich alluvial soil of the Wey. On weekdays throughout the year the general public is allowed to view the splendour at 3s. 6d. a head. Fellows only are allowed in on Sundays. It is a fine place to roam in. You are not herded about and there are plenty of seats for the weary. Go there, especially in spring!

Since becoming established there in 1904, the R.H.S. has gradually extended its grounds, and now, indeed, some of the estate does lie in Wisley parish, a straggly and unhomogeneous grouping of dwellings set mostly on the Bagshot sands that edge the alluvial and perhaps often marshy valley of the Wey. At least the name, Wisley, is supposed to come from the Saxon 'wisc', meaning marshy meadowland, and 'leah', standing for woodland or clearing. The antiquity of the place is proved not just by a mention in Domesday but by the discovery of much neolithic flint and pottery and of Bronze Age pit dwellings in the river sands. At the beginning of this century a fairly complete dugout boat was discovered in the old bed of the Wey, and this, in time, led to many other pre-Roman finds.

Beside the church is a large and prosperous farm with a well-preserved seventeenth-century farmhouse that was once the vicarage. The farm buildings are in fine repair and a visit to the church is accompanied by the satisfied bellowings of at least two 'Big Businesses', if one may refer to *Cold Comfort Farm*!

The church is a small late Norman building, restored in 1872 but retaining much of its original work under some rather drab brownish plaster. Norman windows exist at each side of the chancel, although the east window was inserted into the older framework in about 1600. The round-headed arch of that window still has traces of a painted masonry pattern that may date from its first building. Parts of a painted pattern have been left clear of the whitewash to the right of the altar, and this section looks like a composite cross but is a bit of a four-leaved flower. Outside the chancel arch is another part of the decoration, a painted star. Beside the pulpit is a wrought-iron bracket for an hour-glass, which is sixteenth-century work. The walls are now beginning to peel and the whole building has something of a run-down air. In fact only two services are held here each month, and one feels that the church is hardly representative of a live and vital congregation, unlike the farm just outside.

Not far away is Byfleet, which is quite a different sort of community.

The manor of Byfleet (or Biflet as it was called in Norman times) came into the possession of Edward I, who bequeathed it to his son. The feckless Edward II gave it to his favourite Piers Gaveston and, after the infuriated barons had beheaded Gaveston in 1312, Humphrey de Walden was granted the stewardship, Edward himself continuing to visit and live in the manor as he had done when his friend was resident there. It continued to be royal property throughout late medieval and Tudor times and in 1611 James I gave it to his wife, Anne of Denmark. She began to build a fine house here, which was finished after her death and in due time passed to Henrietta Maria. Evelyn visited it in 1678 but merely described it as a large old building. It remains today as an interesting example of late seventeenth-century domestic architecture, being divided, like so many houses of this period, into three separate dwellings.

Byfleet itself lacks old buildings but has an interesting church, St. Mary's. This is curious in that the main altar is in the north aisle, the centre aisle containing the organ. In the chancel there is a piscina and sedilia with what appear to be squints; there is some pleasant old glass and next to the north window there is a brass of Thomas Teylar, alias Barnby, who died in 1489 having been made rector of Byfleet in 1454 by Henry VI. The living was in crown hands from the reign of Henry III until 1959, with only one very brief interval, and in 1752 Caroline, wife of George II, gave it to a most remarkable man, Stephen Duck. He had been a Wiltshire labourer who had attracted royal attention by his poetry and been made keeper of the Queen's library at Richmond; he learnt Latin in order to take holy orders and was rewarded with the living of Byfleet, but the end of his story was tragic, for in 1756, only two years after his induction, he drowned himself in the Thames in a fit of melancholy.

The pulpit bears the date 1616; older, and the subject of some speculation, are the remnants of wall paintings over and near the south door. A cross is perceptible to the west of the door and above it the painting is said to be of Edward II. It is a far cry from these ancient and unhappily small remains to Victorian musical instruments which stand in cases near by: a flute and a bassoon, the latter having been played in the church orchestra until the organ was put in in 1835. There are two handsome church-wardens' staffs, but much more unusual—indeed almost certainly unique—are the crosses on the south and south-west wall, twenty-five in number. These are the actual crosses which once roughly marked the graves of men who fell in action on the Western Front in the Great War, most of the men thus commemorated having been from Byfleet.

Byfleet has benefited from the construction of a by-pass which takes the traffic away from its main streets. The seventeenth-century iron mill once gave employment to many of the inhabitants, as did the delightfully named 'Mr. Newland's Rosewater and Essential Oil Distillery' which was flourishing at the turn of the century. Nowadays many of the people of Byfleet work in London or in near-by Weybridge and local industry is not greatly prominent.

3

Commuterdom

"THERE runs a road by Merrow Down," wrote Kipling; an ancient road, he meant, a road that has carried mankind from time immemorial. It still runs across the chalk hump from north-east to south-west, from Leatherhead to Guildford, but now it's the A246, a prosaic enough name for what is now a prosaic enough artery that has done its part to bring commuterdom to the old villages of the northern edge of the chalk, where a narrow strip of more fertile soil links the chalk with the London clay. Down there in the clay runs the railway, that other channel bringing men to and from London. The Saxons set their communities on this fertile strip, and their villages struggle still to preserve their integrity amid the shapeless welter of recent building. The church still stands there, wearied maybe with too much restoration, too many simpering stained saints, but proudly peering over the tops of Ferndene, Restharrow, The Oaks, of Dingle Crescent and Manor Way, of Heatherbrow Private Road—No Turning, no L Drivers—and of Martlets Court, these that once were meadows and plough. The pub still stands, too often daubed, extended and mock-Tudorized, alongside a handful of genuine old cottages occasionally even inhabited by genuine old villagers. The basis is there and the basis is even now worth the finding.

Leatherhead has always been a town, long established at the northern end of the Mole Gap. North of it Epsom grew in popularity in the eighteenth century because of the spa waters of the wells and the siting of the racecourse. Beyond Epsom is the sprawl of London. It will not be long before all the villages of this side of the Downs form one long suburb, all originality destroyed.

Ashtead insists still that it is a village. Certainly it was once, and even now, if this is evidence, not one of the major chain stores, except the International, has seen fit to set up shop in The Street. Yet if Ashtead is a village it is in much the same way as a ten-ton elephant still sees itself as a yearling pup, and indeed the old community can still be found in the maze of new roads, the mansions and the semis that make up the present place. Administratively it comes under Leatherhead, as does Bookham, but has grown larger than its senior.

The old parish ran up into the chalk uplands until Headley was detached, and it still has its wide commonland out in the clay. At the time of Domesday, known as Stede, it was an important manor, and before that it seems to have had two Roman villas within its limits, one near the present church and the other away out in the middle of the common. Even in early times, therefore, the wealthy men of the City of London seem to have found it a convenient site for their country estates. Stane Street ran along the chalk about a mile away to the south-east. Perhaps that was why it found favour with the Roman overlords and with their successors.

Apparently the old turnpike road ran along the valley, but a metalled road certainly existed near the present main road. This I know from personal experience, an experience which may fit in here and be found worth the telling.

In the dark days of 1940, in fear of imminent German invasion, many of the able-bodied, not yet conscripted, were set to digging strong points and tank-traps. The professionals were setting up their little machine-gun nests along the ridge of the southern slopes of the Downs. We were digging the crafty second line of defence further back! With several others I was put to work on a defensive post along the old upper road between Leatherhead and Ashtead. We dug, with pick and brawn. It was heavy work, but at last, under the command of our organizer, a major in the local school O.T.C., we had prepared a rather magnificent pit, and we roofed it with corrugated iron and boughs. It was splendidly done. It was then that some representative of the professional army came down to inspect. He was glorious in riding boots and breeches, and he could not have been long out of Sandhurst. He took one look. "What bloody fool," he asked, "sited this damn thing here?" Collapse, as Punch used to say, of amateur military gentleman!

Apart from agriculture—pigs in the forest of the common and sheep on the Downs—Ashtead seems from early times to have had a brick-making industry; the Roman villa on the common bears all the signs of considerable brickworks, the remains of a medieval kiln were all too briefly discovered during the building of Newton Wood Road, and until recently the Ashtead Brick Works were active in Barnett Wood Road.

Before the Conquest the manor of Ashtead was held by Turgis of the Earl Harold. William awarded it to Odo. It passed to the Earl of Surrey and in 1415 it came to the Mowbray family through Elizabeth de Warenne, who married Thomas Mowbray, first Duke of Norfolk. Ultimately it was held by the Howard of Effingham clan. There was also a manor of Little Ashtead, or Priors Farm, held by the Priory of Merton.

Until somewhere in the last century, Ashtead was a rustic, unsophisticated place. Samuel Pepys, who had known it as a boy—"my old place of delight," he called it—was obliged, on one occasion when Epsom could find him no accommodation, to occupy a small room in which he could not stand upright in the house of one Farmer Page. Some few houses of the gentry must have existed, however, even then, although those that still exist of any size, all in Upper Ashtead, all date from after Pepys' day. Ashtead Park, now a school, is a large grey early nineteenth-century mansion. Nearby is what was probably the Dower House, or the agent's residence, an unpretentious but pleasant structure of the seventeenth century, now the headmaster's house. Outside the walls, in Farm Lane, are two fine buildings, Ashtead House of the seventeenth century, with many additions, and a remarkably fine Georgian or Queen Anne frontage, neat and precise, that belongs to Ashtead Park Farm.

Of the ancient church little remains. It is a remarkably attractive building even after reconstructions of 1862 and 1891, but not much of the past remains apart from the sixteenth-century glass in the east window and two small brass inscriptions in the chancel floor, one dated 1590, to John Brown, "late Sargeant of Her Majesty's Wood Yard". There is, it seems, a pre-Conquest window hidden in the building. It is hoped to bring it to view.

The common, however, still retains its past, hidden in the dog-roses and the campion and the bracken that grows upwards of 6 feet tall. Here are the secret relics of the Roman villa and the triangular earthwork that may have been the occupants' last defiance of the later invaders or may just have been their corral for the grazing animals. It is, in any event, a fine place to walk in privacy and dream of the past.

Next to Leatherhead along the south-west sweep of the chalk comes Fetcham, until recently little more than the estate of Fetcham Park, with the great house, the feudal dwellings and the church all closely clustered together. The post-war(s) habitation explosion has now puffed it out into another distended bull-frog of a place. The latest arrivals are encroaching on the old lands of the park as the house slowly disintegrates from its earlier vanity into a pitiable shell, sightless and sullen, beside the church and its own weed-filled drive. Until some six years ago the house was occupied by a tutorial establishment that at least maintained its fabric and gave life to its walls and the good panelling and stair-case inside. Since then, argued about, fought over, discussed but not occupied, it has become a depressing monument to the folly of councils and the unproductiveness of committees.

Fetcham is ancient. It was an early settlement in Saxon times, its name being derived from Fecce's homestead, or the settlement of Fecce's people or family. There is an old local legend that claims that a great battle between Danes and Saxons was fought in A.D. 851 along the ridge here. The discovery of a small Saxon cemetery in the neighbourhood lends some support to the story, but there is no other proof of it. The manor and a church stood here in any case before the Normans came, and the existing church may well contain evidence, materials, sections even, of that old building.

If you look at the outside of the west wall you will see where the original nave must have run and where eighteenth-century additions have extended the line. You will see the Roman bricks that have been utilized in the flintwork and which led to earlier but

now discarded beliefs that the church was set on the site of a
Roman temple. Round the corner, on the south side, beyond the
newer aisle there, stands the square, buttressed tower, late Norman
in its lower part with a later, ornamented upper part, some of the
quoins in stone and some in brick. Most of the long roof is tiled,
but Horsham slabs cover the lower parts.

Most, at least, of the south aisle dates from the twelfth century,
and is much restored, and the arcade is made up of massive Norman pillars with scalloped capitals, and a small round-headed
window still sits above the easternmost pillar. This may be pre-
Conquest work. The south wall of the chancel contains an early
piscina topped by a shelf and inset sedilia in line. In the north
wall is an aumbry. The north aisle and transept were built in the
thirteenth century and the main Gothic arch has some fine, inset,
dog-tooth ornamentation. In the massive southern pillar is the
ancient stairway to the rood screen approached through what may
have been a small Norman arch, set in the north-western corner
of the tower.

Two seventeenth-century memorials are interesting. One is for
Sir Henry Vincent, of the family that owned most of the district
and which will be noted again elsewhere, notably at Stoke d'Abernon. The effigy is of a gentleman in contemporary dress wearing a
ruff and partially painted. The other, on the north wall, is to
Anthony Rous Esquire and is also dated 1631. Underneath is a
finely chiselled little skeleton, doubtless a *memento mori*, with
the additional warning contained in an hour-glass. Apart from the
Saxon cemetery found during building operations on Hawks Hill,
other remains, mostly dating from just before the Roman invasion,
have been discovered in the neighbourhood. Judging from the
Roman tiles in the fabric of the church, there must have been at
least a small villa here. By the time of the Norman Conquest there
were three manors, one held by Edith, the widow of Edward the
Confessor, one listed as being held by one Biga, which passed into
the voracious maw of Odo, and one that by the twelfth century
was held by the Priory of Merton, this fact being still recalled in
the name of Canon (or Canons') Court. All these three manors
came in due course into the control of the d'Abernon family, or to
their successors, the Brays, the Vincents, the Howards.

The manors of Fetcham and Leatherhead came into the keeping, in 1415, of a 9-year-old girl, Anne Croyser, who was the last scion of the d'Abernon family. At the age of 13 she married Ingram Bruyn, who was not too long a'dying, and then she married Sir Henry Norbury, of the family which gave its name to Norbury Park, not far away; she died in 1464. Her son and heir, Sir John, was later Vice-Marshal to Richard III. When the Norbury male line died out, early in the sixteenth century, the estates passed again via the female line to the family of Edmund, Lord Bray. Then, similarly, in 1575, they came to Thomas Vincent and his wife, and, in 1693, to Francis, 5th Baron Howard of Effingham. What vast wealth and power is represented here and switched by a casual touch of fate to new families, new consortia, like business mergers today.

At the beginning of the present century Great and Little Bookham were the subjects of an interesting experiment: a wealthy lady, dedicated to the cause of total abstinence, was engaged in buying up as many inns as came into the market and then suppressing their licences. This well-meant but tactless experiment failed and both the Bookhams today possess a number of inns, notable among them the 'Anchor' and the 'Crown' at Great Bookham and the 'Windsor Castle' at Little Bookham, all of which are historically interesting as buildings.

Bookham appears in Domesday Book as Bockeham where "there are a church and three serfs and a mill of ten shillings and six acres of meadow. There is a wood for eighty fat hogs and thirty lean hogs. Gunfrid holds one hide of this land and he has one plough there."

Nowadays the wood for the fat and the lean swine has doubtless given place to housing estates. Even as these words were written, one of the local Surrey papers described on its front page the opposition raised by the Bookham Residents' Association against a project to make a shopping precinct in the High Street, a narrow but handsome road with a number of good houses and cottages though not, unhappily, the saddlers' shop which once existed there: this has been replaced by a shop with an ultra-modern architecture; thus is progress served.

There is another body in Great Bookham which strives ceaselessly to preserve the village; this is the Community Association, founded in 1949, in order to regain the unity and comradeship created by the stresses and strains of the Second World War. To this association are affiliated all the numerous sports clubs which flourish in the village, including the football club, the stoolball club and the cricket club. The latter had their day of glory in June 1951, when they dismissed their opponents for one run, and that was a leg-bye. Bookham achieved victory by means of four byes so the match was won and lost without a run from the bat! This remarkable affair finds commemoration in no less a place than the pavilion at the Oval where there is a score-card neatly framed behind glass. It is unfortunate that this flourishing club has not got its own ground and must make do with a recreation ground that lacks the facilities upon which village cricket so much depends. It was the Great Bookham Community Association, incidentally, that sponsored the first productions of Shakespeare's plays put on in the lovely grounds of Polesden Lacey House, a mile or so from the village; this house is now National Trust property and its garden and beautifully furnished interior are open to the public.

The centre of village activity, and the working H.Q. of the Community Association, is the fine Elizabethan Barn Hall with its superb original timbers. Attempts are being made to extend this building so as to enhance its value to the village.

Of the church in which presumably Gunfrid and the three serfs worshipped in early Norman times, only two small windows in the north arcade remain, these having been discovered as recently as 1913. The present church, dedicated to Saint Nicholas, is a fine one, not even two restorations, in 1881–5 and in 1885, having managed to destroy its beauty, possibly because the first and major restoration was carried out by the architect who built the superb chapel at Lancing College.

The north aisle was built in 1885 but the narrow south aisle antedates it by more than 700 years; this aisle was divided from the nave by a Norman arcade; over two centuries later the projecting porch, with a priest's room over it, was added, the latter being reached by a circular staircase with upper and lower doors which are still visible, though the priest's room itself disappeared in the nineteenth century.

St. Nicholas was completed in 1341 by John de Rutherwyke, Abbot of Chertsey; the coffin slab now to be seen on the floor north of the altar may be his. It was once in the churchyard near the south door and the studs on it were put there to stop the local boys using it as a slide!

The east window contains six panels of fifteenth-century Flemish glass which was part of a large amount rescued from France during the French Revolution. As extraordinary, though much less decorative than the glass, is the memorial in the chancel to the Andrews family, the tablet being almost surrounded by an enormous representation of a weeping willow. Funerary monuments play a major part in this church and provide a veritable social history in themselves. Apart from the very Victorian weeping willow there are brasses, notably a fine one to Robert Shiers, a lawyer of the Inner Temple, with an inscription in English. Shiers bought the manor of Great Bookham in 1614; his son died without leaving an heir and in 1700 the Rector of Fetcham, Dr. Hugh Shortrudge, acquired the estate; and when he died in 1720 his will gave clear evidence of his high Tory sympathies for he left money to the parsons of four local churches upon condition that they preached an annual sermon commemorating the death of the Anglican 'martyr' Charles I; a Shortrudge sermon is still preached in St. Nicholas on the last Sunday of each January.

Last of the remarkable memorials in the church—though chronologically it comes between the Shiers brass and the weeping willow—is the elaborate one in the north aisle to a certain Thomas Moore who in 1713 obtained the lucrative appointment of paymaster to the English troops stationed at certain European bases. He died unmarried in 1735 at the age of 67, having no doubt enriched himself from his public office as was the custom in the eighteenth century. His memorial lists his virtues at inordinate length and he is characteristically depicted in the costume of ancient Rome, the virtues of which were much esteemed in the England of this time, though very seldom practised.

The Lady Chapel, also called the Slyfield Chapel after the family which lived in the manor house in the sixteenth century, has at its entrance a low screen reconstructed with great skill in 1913 from the remains of a fifteenth-century screen; the parclose screen which separates the chapel from the choir is of the late fifteenth century. There is a fine piscina in the Slyfield Chapel and an east window (perpendicular) whose glass was presented by the niece of Lord Raglan, the commander of the British Army in the Crimean War, where the Christian virtues so painstakingly recorded by his relative were unhappily insufficient to compensate for his almost total lack of basic military skills.

A splendid church, then, in a fine village. The former is no doubt emptier than it was 100 years ago; will men of Surrey 100 years hence be talking regretfully of "Great Bookham, which used to be, we are told, an admirable example of an English village"?

Little Bookham possesses a fine manor house of the eighteenth century, owned for many generations by the Pollen family. They are extensively commemorated in the pleasant little church.

At some time, the Pollens intermarried with the Boileaus who came from France in 1690 in flight from the persecution of their Protestant religion being undertaken by that grossly over-rated monarch, Louis XIV. The Boileau family settled in Norfolk and in Mortlake and their union with the Pollens eventually gave this church a vicar with the splendid name of George Pollen Boileau-Pollen. On the west wall of the church are hatchments of the two families. These hatchments used to be placed over the door of the house in which the dead person had resided; they remained there for about six months and were then put up in the church in which the funeral service had taken place. The examples in Little Bookham are extremely fine, the coats of arms and mottoes being very clear. Above them is a tiny Norman window, the lead font is partly Norman and there are Norman pillars with cushion capitals. It is, in fact, a very fine church, despite its small size and despite the seemingly inevitable Victorian restoration which here perpetrates fresh horrors such as building a hideous pulpit literally around a handsome seventeenth-century wooden one and effectively ruining the east end with a reredos about which charity forbids one to express an opinion. These blemishes detract somewhat from the handsome double piscina and aumbry and from the strong, impressive door to the vestry.

In the churchyard there is a fine old yew, reputed to be as ancient as the church, which may date from the twelfth century, though the first rector listed began his incumbency in 1294. The belfry and spire are timber and the church presents from the outside a most attractive picture especially since it is not on a road but is reached by a narrow lane off the main road.

Effingham was probably the oldest of these settlements, the '-ing-' element being indicative of this. At one time it was certainly the dominant settlement, giving its name to the Hundred and also to the Howards of Effingham family, although it was not until 1551 that Lord William Howard was granted the manor, which previously had been held by Chertsey Abbey and by our old friend, Odo of Bayeux. The other manor of the place was Effingham East Court, awarded by William to another frequenter of these pages, Richard de Tonbridge.

Of all the past nothing now remains, just an odd farmhouse, a cottage or two scattered among the new buildings, and an old pub lavishly traditionalized. The church is hardly even the shell of what it once was owing to a restoration in the last century described by one authority as "remorseless".

Up beyond Effingham lies a line of four villages which were all, at the time of the Conquest in ecclesiastical hands, one of the manors of East Horsley even being held by the Bishop of Exeter. That was Bishop's Manor, and an entry in the Domesday Book recording that "Bishop Osbern of Exeter hold Woking" appears to refer to this manor. This part of the country is included still in the Hundred of Woking, one of those ancient divisions whose original meaning seems to have been lost but which served to cut the country up into manageable administrative areas.

Bishop's Manor continued under the Bishops of Exeter, one of whom, John Bowthe, is commemorated in a handsome little brass, dated 1478, near the altar in the church, until the dangerous days of Henry VIII. It was then sold to the Marquis of Exeter, but he, poor man, played his cards wrongly and the manor was forfeited to the King in 1538. It went speedily through various hands until it was sold in 1584 to Thomas Cornwallis, an official of Queen Elizabeth's court, as may be seen on his tomb in the church. It passed, via the Earl of Southampton, in 1698 to one Denny Muschamp and his wife, the Viscountess Lanesborough, who, from 1701, also held the other East Horsley manor, which had originally been held by the Archbishop of Canterbury for his monks of Christchurch.

Little enough of all its past now remains in East Horsley. It is an enormous and very respectable residential area, expensive, smooth and making valiant efforts to retain some sort of historical unity, whether it be by the line of mock-Tudor, but well-built mock-Tudor, shops, or by the wrought-iron name-signs that stand at crossroads.

Perhaps this tendency was begun in the eighteen-twenties by Sir Charles Barry, the architect of the 'Gothic' Houses of Parliament, who designed here an 'Elizabethan' mansion complete with Great Hall and Minstrels' Gallery. The house that was built from his plans was sold, only ten years later, to the Lord King who was soon to be created Earl of Lovelace, and whose forebear has a fine Baroque tomb in Ockham church. This Lord King was something of a civil engineer and architect, and he redesigned the house and rebuilt it in the astonishing form it has today.

This is Horsley Towers, now a training establishment of the Central Electricity Authority, and it is worth a visit, an as example of what a florid and wealthy imagination run riot can produce. There is a unifying use of decorative brickwork that runs from the lodges through the gateway and past the stables and the cottages where the ruddy-cheeked retainers should be touching forelocks, and through a 50-yard tunnel up to the mansion. There are decorated towers that would do credit to mad King Ludwig, overlooking a small lake surrounded with great firs and cedars, and over the last arch before the main courtyard is the private chapel. This is a psychedelic amalgam of the Sainte Chapelle in Paris, a Baroque creation in Anatolia and some kind of bastard Byzantine oratory, a confection of coloured bricks and tiles, of glaring glass in windows of keyhole design, a splendidly ridiculous folly that is quite delightful.

The church of East Horsley has a magnificent early Norman tower, a massive structure in three stages, the topmost of which, unfortunately, has been, since the eighteenth century, covered with a nasty battlemented thing in poor-quality brick and daubed over

Row of cottages at Blechingley

Blechingley

The village green at Brockham

An alabaster carving in the porch of Abinger Church

Abinger: *(above)* the motte and church, *(below)* morris dancing at the medieval fair

with brownish stucco. There is a tiny Norman window on the west
side, just above the twelfth-century opening. On the south side,
above the lancet is a small tile-lined opening that led to a flue that
connected with a fireplace, possibly in a room previously used by
the priest. The great buttresses were set there in the fourteenth
century and the oldest of the bells dates from 1450.

The interior has considerable appeal, even though a restoration
in 1869 made some unfortunate alterations, remodelled the chancel
and raised its floor, inserted windows and typical stained glass,
removed a seventeenth-century pulpit and imposed the Victorian
flamboyant cage that stands there now. In spite of all this, and in
spite of the present organ, the whole effect is pleasant, spacious,
cool and beautifully kept and decorated with flowers. There are
several interesting memorials; on the north wall of the chapel
is a brass of John Snellyng and his wife, Alys, with, below, their
six sons and five daughters. Opposite, on the south wall of the
nave, there is a brass commemorating their son, Thomas, here
spelled Snellinge, and his wife Jone, and their thirteen offspring.
The earlier brass is dated 1489 and the later 1504, and between
them, the word soul is rendered as "sowllis", "soulis" and
"soules", "sowlys", no mean scriptorial performance!

On the west of the chancel arch is a fourteenth-century brass of
Robert de Brentyngham, a priest, and on the floor to the left of the
altar a very finely executed brass of John Bowthe, in vestments,
with mitre and crozier, dated 1478.

In the north aisle stands the tomb of Thomas Cornwallis, "some-
time Pentioner and Groome Porter to Queen Elizabeth of Blessed
Memory" and to his wife, Lady Katherine, the daughter of the
Earl of Southampton. The two figures in marble lie on the tomb,
and, beside them, are their two children, one now lacking a head.

In all it is a pleasant church to visit because it is obviously so
lovingly cared for, so spotless and welcoming.

When we first visited the church of East Horsley on its slight
knoll south of the main Leatherhead-Guildford road, it was under-
going repairs necessitated by the havoc caused by woodworm and
death watch beetle. On a later visit, the building had been restored
to use; though it was locked because of vandalism, the key could be
obtained at the vicarage.

E

This handsome church has Saxon east and west walls, late Norman north pillars and arcade and late Tudor south pillars and arcade. The chancel arch dates from 1210, the wooden screen from 1470. The probable entrance to the rood loft can be seen to the left of the chancel arch and below this is the parish chest of 1240. The pulpit is the top portion of a former three-decker.

The sanctuary has some ancient glass: the effigy of Sir James Berners in the north side window is about 1384, the lancets in the east window are about 1210, with original glass in the north and middle lights' roundels. Under the north window is a stone effigy of a priest who may be Ralph Berners; he died in 1348 (of plague?). The remains of a stone coffin are in the sanctuary north wall and on the south side of the chancel there is part of a fourteenth-century alabaster. Two large eighteenth-century monuments in the south chapel are now masked by the organ. Walter Raleigh's head is said to be buried under the floor of this chapel: it had been given to his widow whose hope that it would be buried with his body came to nothing so it was interred with his son's body when the latter died in 1680. The Raleighs held West Horsley Place only after 1643 and it soon passed to Sir Edward Nicholas whose long political career ended when he was Secretary of State to Charles II. His son had a terrible experience in the great storm of 1703 when a chimney fell into his bedroom and killed his wife. He was then 80 years old and it is not surprising that he survived this tragedy by less than a year.

The eastern triptych of the church, to the right of the altar in the north chapel, should be noted, while the north doorway is a fine example of late twelfth-century work; the door itself is 200 years later. On the west wall are traces of medieval murals depicting the Fall of Man. The tower doorway is late Norman, the tower itself is of 1120.

This is such a good church that it is surprising to find that it was twice restored in the nineteenth century; Ogilvy found it in the hands of workmen—as we did—when he visited it just before the Great War. He found "a tall, deft-fingered sculptor replacing the broken portions of the recumbent figure on an ancient tomb". Ogilvy queried the accuracy of the ascription of this tomb, doubting whether the long-haired, untonsured figure could be the priest

Roger or Ralph de Berners. Ogilvy also doubts whether the glass does represent Sir James Berners, one of the favourites of Richard II executed in Bristol or London when the king fell from power.

Beyond the Horsleys come the Clandons; the word derives from the Anglo-Saxon 'cleane dun', or clean down, an easy one for the philologist, because here were bare sweeps of chalk. From earliest times the manor of East Clandon was held by the great Abbey of Chertsey and from the eleventh to the fourteenth century the village was called Clandon Abbatis. It is mentioned definitely as being held by Chertsey in a copy of the charter drawn up in A.D. 727, and it is believed that it formed part of the original gift when the Abbey was founded in, or about, A.D. 675. It was so held in Domesday, but during Henry VIII's absorption of church lands it fell to the royal authority in 1537. After various changes of ownership it came, in 1718, to Sir Peter King and so, in the nineteenth century, to the Earl of Lovelace, who has already appeared in these pages.

One remarkable feature of feudal times was that this manor was entirely tenanted by small farmers, or villeins, without there being a central manorial estate or demesne. Very few manors existed with this arrangement in medieval England. This kind of holding, with considerable common lands, lasted until the days of the King family, and enclosure of these common lands, permitted now by law, brought an end to this freedom between 1794 and 1809.

Round the church are several good, though restored and modernized, cottages which give the setting an unusual charm. The old manor lies back behind the church, a solid late seventeenth- or early eighteenth-century farm house, and just up the road is the Old Forge, in which some of the ancient building can be discerned.

Some parts of the church show the Norman foundations of the building of 1110, but what must have been a cramped nave and small, possibly apse-shaped, chancel was enlarged about 1220 and the north aisle built a little later. It is worth noticing the huge pillars that anchor the arcade and which seem to be half-buried to increase their power. The curious decoration of the north aisle came about in 1913 when the Rendel tomb was installed and the vestry added at the west end. The communion rail and panelling are of the latter part of the seventeenth century. There is not much else to mention except, perhaps, the six hatchments, three over the chancel arch and three at the west end. Really the church looks more inviting than it is, perhaps because of the rather pleasant setting.

Not far from the church is the noble parkland of Hatchlands, now a National Trust property. The house was built about the middle of the eighteenth century by Admiral Boscawen "at the expense", it was said, "of the enemies of his country", a reference, no doubt, to the amount of prize-money he obtained from the French, whom he defeated in the now forgotten battle of Louisberg in 1758. The house is rather plain, in red brick, with an oriel in the centre of the front. Part of the interior was decorated by the rising young Robert Adam.

J. S. Ogilvy tells a good story about an old countryman whom he met near West Clandon just before the Great War. This aged inhabitant was advising the rain-soaked author to take a glass of old ale and deploring the tendency of some people to drink lemonade. This nauseous drink, he affirmed, had been responsible for a distressing happening to an old lady of his acquaintance: understandably proud of having cut a new set of teeth when in her eighties, she had been prevailed upon, on a hot summer day, to drink some lemonade, whereupon "her teeth were all melted away". In disappointment she took to her bed and died less than three weeks later!

West Clandon preserves another ancient legend, because in the porch of its church there is a reproduction of a medieval carving depicting a dog with the head of a dragon in its mouth. The legend runs that once upon a time the people of West Clandon were terrified by a dragon which inhabited Send Marsh to the north of the village. A soldier who had deserted from the army appeared in the village with his dog and promised to kill the dragon if the villagers would procure him a pardon for his desertion. The bargain was struck, he departed for the Marsh and his brave dog seized the dragon's head which the soldier struck off with the sword; he then returned to the village and the inhabitants kept their part of the bargain. As is the way with all best legends, there is a disarming vagueness about this one, neither its date nor the names of its protagonists being known.

It is unfortunate that little of the twelfth-century church has been preserved, while in 1874 restorers tore out the Jacobean carved pulpit and the minstrels' gallery and ruined the font, which still then had its twelfth-century bowl. In 1716 restoration had taken place to make good damage caused by the falling in of the roof; the ancient timbers were skilfully used and are still visible, the Victorians having neither destroyed them nor covered them with a tasteful layer of varnish.

The church is rather a hotch-potch, with some fine things like the wooden painting in the chancel showing St. Thomas of Canterbury between St. Peter and St. Paul, the aumbry and piscinas in the chancel, the holy-water stoop (though mutilated) by the south door and the finely carved pews at the back of the nave, Spanish or Austrian work of the early eighteenth century in all probability. These were presented by a member of the Onslow family which had its country seat at West Clandon after 1642 when Richard, who had had the dubious distinction of being knighted by James I, bought it from Sir Richard West.

The church's windows include the small lancet of the mid-thirteenth century in the chancel and the large east window, a century younger. The north and south doorways are mid-twelfth century but the tower was restored in 1914 after a fire. The mass-clock on the outer south wall bears the date 1180.

Clandon Park stretches out between West Clandon and Merrow. The Onslow family had this as their headquarters from 1642, re-building the mansion, the designs being by Giacomo Leoni, a Venetian architect, in Palladian style in the 1730s. It is a large and ornate red-brick building and is owned by the National Trust. At the time of writing it is closed to the public because of reconstruction work.

Of Merrow itself we expect more than it offers, probably because of Kipling. It was clearly a Saxon community and its name seems to refer to the meres or pools that once existed down towards the river, and perhaps, too, to the yew trees on the chalk. It had its mention in Domesday. There are some old cottages almost all hidden behind modern shop fronts or acres of later façadery. Even the 'Horse and Groom' that proudly advertises its date as 1615 has little enough of its original structure to show.

The church stands out handsomely by the roadside but even that was almost wholly rebuilt in 1843. There are some fine things in it, a good Gothic barge board on the porch, some late Norman pillars between the nave and the south aisle, these bearing some scratched Pilgrim crosses, and a very fine ancient lectern carved with a Bacchic design containing a god and grapes. If you want to go in you have to fetch the key from a shop the other side of the turmoil of the A246, and then you wonder if it was worth the risk!

To the north-west of Leatherhead, after bursting through the Dorking Gap in the chalk, the Mole struggles its way through the London clay. This meandering route at this stage is partly responsible for its name; the rest is owed to its habit, in the gap, of burrowing through the chalk crust to form the so-called Swallow Holes, mentioned elsewhere. As it approaches Cobham, its meanders become even more violent in the vicinity of Stoke d'Abernon where an outlying region of Claygate gravel lies on top of the clay and runs back to form Oxshott Heath. Here the river cuts an almost rectangular course, veering south and back again. Where it turns southward the defensive post of Stoke—for that is what the name means—was established at some period as yet unknown. The site overlooked the ancient ford.

At the time of Edward the Confessor the manor of Stoke was held by a powerful supporter of the King, named Brixi or Brisci Cild, whose name is also remembered in Brixton. From the use of Roman bricks and even of Roman cornices in the fabric of the church, it is clear that there must have been a Roman settlement at this point. How much earlier it came into being is something that has yet to be established. It seems, in any case, that a church was built here not long after St. Augustine brought the Christian faith to these islands in 597. Estimates vary, of course, but the fact is that certainly some of the existing building was set there before the Normans came, and that this is one of the first churches to be built in this part of England.

It is a good site; along the river banks, especially on the south side, the alluvial land is fertile, a fat and prosperous land for agriculture. It still is, and because the land is easily flooded, it has not yet fallen into the hands of the estate developers as has the gravel height to the north. Only some rugby grounds break the area between the church and the railway, beyond which a layer of gravel soil has created the inevitable urbanization.

The church is remarkable, beautiful, astonishing, in spite of a restoration in 1866 by Ford and Hesketh, described by the writer in the Collins Guide as "destructive". As a result of this "representation of reality", to misuse Cézanne's phrase, the exterior of the building has little interest, although it is superbly placed beside the river. There is a chic little tower at the west end, and there is a romantic coat of arms on the north-east corner. A Saxon sundial that had been mounted on the refurbished south wall collapsed in 1933, and was then rebuilt there. The south wall, in fact, shows much of essence of the church; far less harm was done here. The shape of the antique building can be seen and it is possible to visualize the Saxon nave and apse. The Roman bricks utilized in the construction are visible, as is the old blocked doorway, square-headed and utilitarian, some 12 feet above the ground, which served at one time to provide entrance for the lord of the manor to his special private, raised, 'box' or thegn's gallery. This is the earliest English example of such a structure because, in general, these oldest churches were all of collegiate foundation and not, as this is, a manorial place of worship.

Before 1866 the Saxon tall and narrow arch to the chancel still stood, even when the chancel was rebuilt in its present rectangular form in the thirteenth century. The new chapel provided the nobility with its own chapel behind the altar which would have stood only just to the eastward of the chancel arch. The stone bench that runs the length of the south wall of the chancel was a part of the furnishing for this private church-going.

The chancel and sanctuary contain so many exciting things that they would almost be a museum or art gallery, if they were not the centre of a living religion. The most famous feature is the pair of great brasses on the floor in front of the massive and seventeenth-century altar rails. The larger of these two brasses, on its original slab, is the oldest memorial brass in England, a wonderfully preserved figure, more than 6 feet tall, of Sir John d'Abernon, a piece of fine craftsmanship dating from 1277. There he lies now, a daunting figure in all his height, legs straight, dressed in chain mail and surcoat, a lance held in his crooked arm on his right, his shield, still enamelled blue, on his left, his feet lying pointed on the heraldic lion.

Beside him lies his son, another Sir John, below a smaller, less ornate effigy. He died in 1327 and is shown wearing the armour of his day where chain mail is reinforced with some plate armour and greaves. He has no lance and his shield is uncoloured. On the other side of the elder Sir John is Sir John III, but he has no portrait in brass, only several small shields, one of which at least, the one that has the d'Abernon chevron arms surmounted by the four stripes of the eldest son, is but a replica of the original, this one stolen in 1916. A few letters of the mortuary inscription in the stone can be discerned by the keen-eyed.

In the thirteenth-century rebuilding some parts of the original Saxon apse were incorporated, notably in the south wall, which had to be thickened and strengthened to support the weight of the fine stone vaulting. There was, it seems, no east window then— that was introduced in the next century—and a mural painting filled that wall. A small section of this can be seen today, four panels displaying the musical accompaniment to what was a scene of the Adoration of the Lamb. The east window, fortunately free of Victorian stained glass, contains a number of panels and roundels of fourteenth- and fifteenth-century glass, mainly Flemish, set sensibly in clear surrounds. There are also two small lancets in the south wall equally holding early glass sections. At the side of that nearest the chancel arch is another piece of wall-painting, a rough faded ochre design of tendrils and leafage.

Over the altar hangs a magnificent fifteenth-century painting of the Annunciation, a superb example of its period and style, a scene filled with that love of realism, details of family life and architecture that show the simple certainty of the artist that such events could happen in his own day and in his own home. All the furnishings of the sanctuary, too, are splendidly assorted pieces, chairs, stool credence table, aumbry on the wall, the altar itself under its drapery, all of the seventeenth century.

There is also a very fine pulpit, late Elizabethan or early Jacobean, almost unique of its kind in the country, dark, almost black, very tall with its great sounding-board suspended from iron stays wrought in Surrey or Sussex, and ornately carved, with lions' heads and what look like Romans supporting it at the corners. Nearby is a stalwart wooden chest with three geometrical designs carved on the front. In the lid is a slit for coins and inside is a receiving tray, all put there, it is believed, when the chest was made, perhaps in 1210, to collect donations for the Crusade. The lectern is Caroline, as is the suggestive hour-glass next to the pulpit.

The nave has a simple hammer-beam roof, and in the south wall, near the present door, can be seen the blocked-in doorway, 12 feet up, for the thegn's gallery. About the middle of that wall is the blocked-in doorway that was the main entrance until the nineteenth-century restoration. Outside you will see a fifteenth-century holy-water stoup, much degraded.

The north aisle was built towards the end of the twelfth century and one Norman pillar remains with some pilgrims' crosses scratched into its lower part and a just discernible crucifix in faded paint.

The Norbury Chantry chapel was built about 1490 by Sir John Norbury, to whose family the estates had passed in 1464, as so often, by the female line. It is held that the chantry may have been a thank-offering for his surviving the Battle of Bosworth. A pair of seventeenth-century Italian wrought-iron gates separates the chapel from the aisle, and in the massive pillar where they are set climb the old stairs to the rood-loft now disappeared. Between the chapel and the sanctuary is a shapely Tudor arch, in which, at one time, Sir John's tomb must have stood. It is now occupied by the tomb of a thirteenth-century rector, Sir Richard the Little, according to the epitaph.

On the eastern side of the arch has been placed a small brass, formerly on the floor, of Anne Norbury. It was she who, at the age of 13, had inherited all the d'Abernon estates and who, *en secondes noces*, had married Sir Henry Norbury and was Sir John's mother. Pictured in the folds of her skirt are her offspring, four boys and four girls. Beside her, on the wall, is a fragment of an angel, the only survival, it appears, of Sir John's tomb, described as an "ould monument being by injury of time demolisht".

Under that is an amusing little rotund figure, thought to be that of an Elizabethan child from some funerary statue. On the Western side of the arch is the small brass effigy of a child in swaddling clothes, Ellen Bray, who died in 1516 within a month of her baptism. By female line again, the Norbury estates had by then passed to Edmund, Lord Bray.

Later still, in similar fashion, the estates passed to the Vincents, one of whom, Thomas, was knighted by Queen Elizabeth, who came to Stoke d'Abernon to perform this office and was doubtless entertained at considerable expense at the manor house, this in 1590. Several members of the Vincent family have their monuments in the chantry, all rather splendid though somewhat sombrely dressed in early seventeenth-century costume, several perkily perched on one elbow. In the east window are coats of arms of the families of the succession from the d'Abernons to the Vincents, and near the entrance is a wide Tudor fireplace that shows either that noble families were not unwilling to cosset themselves even in church or that the chapel was once used as a schoolroom.

In modern times it seems, from the references, that Conan Doyle's adventure of "The Speckled Band" took place at a house here.

4

The Downs

CHALK is porous, drains easily, dries quickly. This makes it good for horse-race tracks and even for sports fields, but not so good for agriculture, apart from providing grazing land for sheep. Most of the parishes along both edges of the Downs extend quite a long way up on to the chalk. Names like Sheep Leas, above Horsley, explain clearly the usage and the value of these chalk-lands.

After the Norman Conquest there were very few settlements on the chalk hills, and the whole district became an enormous hunting area, closely preserved for the king's use and subject to the very harsh forest laws, which were administered quite separately from, and over-rode, the established laws of the land. The existence of this forest range is attested by many of the present place-names: Kingswood, Buckland, Hartswood, Warren Farm, Hallelu Farm (derived from the old French 'Hallali', a hunting term for death, and 'halloo', used to urge on the hounds). Naturally enough there were very few communities established in this forest. There was no means of livelihood for anyone not connected with the hunting itself, and only death for anyone who poached the royal game. No one, therefore, would ever want to settle there unless he were some part of the organization, a verderer or a parker. It probably the latter official, who, because of the prying and spying nature of his job, brought into being the character called 'Nosey'.

It is only since the coming of the railways that the Downs have become widely populated, and even now the townships cling, like a parasite growth, to the arteries of travel. Away from the main roads and railways, even within some 15 miles from Charing Cross, the communities are often tiny, remote, secret, unsophisticated, rustic, tucked away along narrow country roads. Their churches are, in many cases, a long way from the village and probably grew up first in either the confines of a castle or as a chapel of ease for travellers along the so-called Pilgrims' Way or for the huntsmen themselves.

Remains of Roman villas have been found along the southern edge of the chalk-lands here but such civilization as they brought mostly disappeared in subsequent centuries.

The 1965 reorganization of the county boundaries left three villages tucked away in the easternmost corner of Surrey on the shore-line of the extended sea of Greater London. The first of these is Chelsham, a dull collection of newish houses just on the edge of booming Warlingham. The chalk is covered by a layer of clay-with-flints and, within the parish, is an isolated island of gravel. There has been some extraction of the gravel, and at one time there was digging for that curious pink stone with white spots, known technically as Breccia and familiarly as plum-pudding stone. Some rudimentary earthworks or trenches in the district suggest some earlier, unknown history for the place. At the Conquest it was awarded to the omnivorous Richard de Tonbridge. From him it passed, in due course, through the Despensers, the Beauchamps and the Nevills to Anne, the wife of Richard, Duke of Gloucester, who became Shakespeare's tyrant king, Richard III. In the fourteenth century there were two small-holdings in the manor with the delightful names of Bednestede and Fickleshole. Beddlestead still exists in the middle of the country along the narrow road that leads south towards Titsey.

The church stands over a mile away to the east. It occupies a fine position amid great trees, but is mainly a restoration of 1871. This is not to say that it lacks dignity or grace. Indeed it is a handsome building outside and it is lovingly tended within. The original chapel, which came under Warlingham, was quite likely a late Norman building, and the existing font probably came from that period, though it has later been set on four miserable little shafts. It seems that some major reconstruction was carried out at the end of the thirteenth century, when the north wall of the nave was rebuilt with the present windows and the chancel remodelled. There is still the piscina of that time, standing out from the wall on a foliate corbel. In the south corner is a short shaft, thought to have been part of the sedilia destroyed in the eighteenth century, and the lancet windows are also of the thirteenth century, as is the tower with the arch leading from the nave. The exterior of the tower was adorned, in 1871, with spire, parapet, and buttresses.

Chelsham sits in some splendid downland scenery, and you can walk or drive over green, rolling uplands in every direction, except perhaps to the north. Farms and rich estates are plentiful, as, doubtless, they have been for centuries. Southwards there is nothing before Titsey, which clings to the southern slope of the Downs, and is only partly perched on the chalk.

J. L. Pearson is one of the indefatigable Victorian architects whose work is found all over Surrey. One of his earlier designs was that for the new church at Titsey, which was built in 1861, in Early English style. The old church had stood close to the manor house, but the lord of the manor of that time had objected to its being so near his home and had ordered its destruction. So a new church had to be built outside the fences of the estate. It stands just across the way from a solid seventeenth-century farmhouse, Titsey Court, and beside a long building dated 1673, once the Grasshopper Inn and now called Church Cottage. Titsey Place, the manor house, keeps itself securely tucked away behind a screen of trees and fierce demands for privacy. Even the old building hides behind a nineteenth-century façade.

Remains of a Roman villa were found in the grounds of the Place, but there is nothing to see there now; removable relics went to the museum at Guildford, and the rest has been taken over by the stinging nettles. The Roman owners established, apparently, a fulling industry there, but now it is only an agricultural estate, dull and secretive.

The great primitve east-west trackway ran along the Downs just above Titsey, and there is a farm called Pilgrims' Lodge nearby. This may mark a stopping place for the medieval pilgrims, but more probably it represents a romantic idea conceived by some previous owner. The church at Tatsfield, however, was probably established as a chapel of ease for pilgrims; its position is much closer to the trackway than to the existing village.

Tatsfield is a very small village indeed and might not have found its way into this book but for its delightful little church and the marvellous view from the churchyard. This church has the unusual characteristic that it is used for Anglican and Roman Catholic services, and another interesting point about it is that it claims to be the highest church in the county, being nearly 780 feet above sea level.

It is a Norman church built about 1075; it has had two restorations, the first in 1838 (rather earlier than is the case with most Surrey village churches) and again as recently as 1966/67. The most obvious Norman remnants—apart, of course, from the walls themselves—are the two small windows on the north side of the nave. The chancel was rebuilt in 1330, though the firestone arch dividing it from the nave is a century older. The east window contains some ancient glass and in the chancel also are two fine Early English windows, an unusual piscina and an exceptionally large aumbry.

Notice on the north wall the copy of a Rubens painting of the Crucifixion, the original being in Antwerp; the hatchment over the chancel arch is of the Leveson-Gower family who still are patrons of the living.

On the south wall there is an interesting early eighteenth-century monument to Alice and John Corbett; he was a carpenter, "a person truly ingenious", and his son put up the monument, giving the church also an altar-piece and a royal coat of arms, both of which have unhappily been lost. In the churchyard is a gravestone of a certain Timothy Burgess with this admonitory epitaph:

> Once I stood as you do now,
> And gaz'd o'er them as you do me,
> And you will lie as I do now,
> While others thus look down on thee.

The view from this churchyard is really superb: over to the left is Kent and the country round Sevenoaks, directly south is Limpsfield and, beyond it, the high ground near East Grinstead; to the right can be seen the spire of Titsey church and Oxted. One of the best things about this superb view is that it is unspoilt by such modern accretions as pylons; not very far from Tatsfield church, however, there are ominous signs of a new motorway under construction. Ominous is, perhaps, the wrong adjective to use, for this road, running as it will, along the crest of the Downs, will relieve the pressure of traffic in the valley and make the A25 less of a threat than it is at present to villages like Blechingley and Oxted.

A noisy, crowded road, the A23, cuts Merstham in half and makes the crossing of the village's main street a hazardous affair. Yet, only a few yards away from the thundering lorries, is one of the most delightful streets in Surrey, aptly named Quality Street. This name is not, in fact, a tribute to the houses in the street but was given simply because Sir Seymour Hicks, the actor, once lived here when playing in Barrie's *Quality Street*. There are not many dwellings in this wide but short street but each is a gem: note particularly on the right-hand side, halfway up, The Old Forge, a fifteenth-century building most skilfully restored. Court Cottage, Prior's Mead and Mead Cottages, the Old Manor and the Old School House are almost as delightful as The Old Forge.

Merstham has a Battle Bridge and an Oakley Wood. Some locals claim it as the site of the famous battle between the Saxons and the Danes, but this claim is flimsy. What cannot be disputed is Merstham's possession of what may well be the oldest public railway in England. This was the Croydon, Merstham and Godstone Iron Railway, which worked by horse traction and began its operations in 1803 (from Wandsworth to Croydon) and from 1805 was extended here. In 1951 the Surrey County Council set up part of the original line on a site next door to the 'Jolliffe Arms' in Brighton Road and this site should be a 'must' for all students and lovers of railways.

Merstham had famous quarries of sandstone which was in great demand for London buildings, including Henry VII's chapel in Westminster Abbey and, later, London Bridge.

There is a footpath leading from the top end of Quality Street to the parish church, dedicated to St. Katherine. This is built of the local sandstone and stands most attractively at the top of a tree-decorated knoll. Of the earliest church on this site only the chancel arch remains and this is late twelfth century; the Sussex marble font, however, is also twelfth century. The church we see today is basically a thirteenth-century building, much restored in the nineteenth century. The west door, with its keyhole arch and dogtooth moulding, is thirteenth century and the shingled spire is one century later. In the chantry, the east window has some old glass at its top and there are brasses here and in the main chancel. The table-tomb of John Elingbridge has suggestively his two wives in effigy upon it but his own brass is missing; near the altar in the north chapel is a brass of John Ballard and his wife (1463) and in the north aisle is an effigy which was at one time used as a paving stone in the north chapel and which represents a fifteenth-century merchant.

There are more recent memorials to members of the Jolliffe family. Lieutenant George Jolliffe was a young naval officer killed in 1798 at the Battle of the Nile, and four years later his father William died "the victim of a casualty as aweful as unforeseen". An unlucky family at that period of its history.

The mosaic floor in this north chantry chapel was apparently made by the notorious Constance Kent while in prison, and the fact that she found such meritorious employment would no doubt have pleased a former rector of Merstham, the famous humanist and doctor, Thomas Linacre, one of the group of scholars who were ornaments of the court of Henry VII and friends of the great Erasmus. He was rector of Merstham in 1509. The rectory, opposite the church, is a most handsome eighteenth-century house with a large garden; the rector is responsible also for Gatton and, since Merstham is a place that has grown very considerably in recent years, he is a very busy man. Unhappily, St. Katherine's at Merstham and the church at Gatton have to be kept locked because of repeated acts of vandalism.

Gatton is shy. It took us three separate attempts before we found our way there. There seems to be no signpost that directs you to the village centre, if that is the right word—to the town hall, at least, and the town hall is in the official list of Surrey antiquities. The Victoria County History, dated 1911, says this: "There is no

The Norman doorway of Shere Church

Chilworth Manor

Shalford Mill

Cottages at Hambledon

Winkworth Farm, Hascombe

St. Bartholomew's Church, Wanborough

Waverley Abbey

shop, no public-house, and now no school. There are five gentle-men's houses, one vacant, besides Gatton Park and the Rectory, and one farm." There are references along the roads nearby; Gat-ton Bottom, you will find, and even Upper Gatton. But the church? And the town hall?

Well, it does exist. Go north up the A23 from Redhill and turn up Rocky Lane, just on the outskirts of Merstham. When you come to a white gate with the notice 'Private Road', turn in, and, amid a lot of modern school buildings, you will find the park, with a splendid classical portico and a small notice that says 'House-mistress', and, to the side, the church. If you are approaching along the old trackway called on the maps the 'Pilgrims' Way' turn up along a road signposted the 'Royal Alexandra and Albert School', and you will reach the same white gate. For that is what this magnificent park has become, and magnificently it is main-tained for the benefit of some 500 children, most of whom are orphans. The terrace looks out over a vast lake to an enormous expanse of the country of the Weald. This must be one of the finest views in the county.

It is an old manor—under Edward the Confessor it was assessed at ten hides—but it seems never to have been anything other than a hunting estate, although the origin of the name suggests that it was a farm where goats were kept. In 1332 there were seventeen in-habitants, and until now (when the school is not in residence at least) there have seldom been more. And yet, in 1452 it received the privilege of sending two burgesses to Parliament, and no one seems to know why. The manor was a small part of the widespread holdings of the powerful Arundel-Norfolk consortium, and just before achieving its borough status it had passed, in sub-fee, to a family called Copley. The Copleys were clearly staunch Catholics and remained so, to their discomfort, in the dangerous ages to come. It is possible therefore to see the strong Howard hand be-hind the award of borough status to this tiny manor.

In 1539 Sir Roger Copley, still in possession, found the privilege of electing the two members 'burdensome', because there was only one house to be of any help in paying the members' wages.

By the middle of the eighteenth century the manor was held by Sir James Colebrooke, and he goes down in history as the man who

F

had the great lake constructed by damming the streams and who had all the old monuments in the church cleared out and destroyed. He is reputed to have used the church as a storehouse for the farm.

Early in the nineteenth century the park was acquired by John, 5th Baron Monson, and he set to work to repair the ravages of his predecessor. He scoured Europe for fittings for the church. It was a good time for fine pickings, a time when various revolutionary movements shook the Continent and radical administrations were prepared to sell off ecclesiastical treasures with an eye only to their secular values. Gatton church was turned into a museum of wonderful things. Report has it that the Baron impoverished himself in the process. Certainly the seventh Baron, first Viscount Oxenbridge, sold the estates in 1888 to Jeremiah Colman, the mustard king.

It is certainly reasonable that the church should be kept locked, not only because of the vandalism that seems to be rife in this part of the world, but also because Gatton is, outside Oxford and Cambridge, unique. It is arranged like a college chapel with stalls, from a Benedictine monastery in Ghent, facing inwards and sideways to the altar. These stalls are carved with cherubs' heads and they have misericords carved, not very interestingly, with heads and foliage designs. The pulpit is set high above and consists of some wonderfully deeply carved panels of the descent from the Cross. Although their attribution to Albrecht Dürer himself is doubtful, they are magnificent. They were once in a reredos in Nuremburg, and a further part, showing the women at the foot of the Cross, makes up the front of the altar table.

The panels of the chancel-surrounds are old French Gothic from Burgundy cunningly set in modern framing. The topmost line is a series of beautifully carved designs. The canopies and the wainscotting behind the stalls in the nave came from the Cathedral of Aurschot in Louvain, and are carved in elaborate, delicate tracery. At the west end is a glorious parclose screen that was obtained from some unnamed thirteenth-century English church, and, finally, the heavy communion rail came from Tongres in Flanders. What an array of superlative woodwork and how royally it all fits together!

And this is not the whole list of the treasures of this place. The glass here does not, as so often, detract from the total impact; it consists mostly of pieces of fifteenth-century work carefully pieced together to create a coherent pattern. The west window glows with the arms of Henry VII supported by a red dragon and a greyhound. The font, patched though it is, belongs to the original church, as does the aumbry in the chapel, both probably of the twelfth century.

Not far from the church, standing in a small grove of great trees, is the 'Town Hall', a handsome ring of slender pillars in Classical style, roofed to form a sort of open portico. Beside it is a giant urn raised "in memory of the deceased borough". It is perhaps a little ironic that a memorial in the style of ancient Greece, the cradle of democracy, should commemorate the election by, at best, three voters of two members of Parliament!

There is really nothing more to tell about Gatton, but it is hard to resist the temptation to record the name of one of the earlier lords of the manor. It is one that Shakespeare might have delighted to use for one of Sir Toby Belch's companions, or Goldsmith or any of the Restoration writers in any of their comedies. He was Sir William Milksop, knight, Lord of the Manor in 1301.

On the chalk heights above the Coulsdon valley is the straggling village of Chipstead which is now only just inside the borders of Surrey after the recent changes. Chipstead is now a sizeable place, yet less than half a century ago an account of its church was preceded by the words "there is no village"; so the numerous—and often very handsome—houses which are now the homes of commuters have all sprung up since the end of the Great War. The church, however, is very old. The Norman doorway in the north wall dates from 1180 and it is possible that the nave is even more ancient. The tower and its fine vaulting, the chancel, the north transept and the south aisle are early thirteenth century but the square-headed window opening in the latter is much earlier. In the chancel are two stone benches, curiously carved at their ends, and the east window contains some old glass, as does the south window of the south transept. The chancel has nine lancet windows, triangular-headed, and, extremely unusual, a piscina and two stalls which face the altar, rather in the fashion of collegiate chapels.

The screen is fifteenth century, the pulpit a skilful assembly of the remains of a Jacobean pulpit, the font fourteenth century. An exceptionally handsome doorway leads into the north transept where there might have been a chantry chapel as it has a piscina.

The modern parts of this church—the north aisle and arcade and the south transept—blend in well with the older portions and though there were several restorations during the nineteenth century the antiquity of the building was not seriously affected by these.

In the churchyard there is the tomb of Sir Edward Banks (who has a monument in the church itself) whose career provides a perfect example of that transformation from rags to riches which so delighted Victorian moralists like Samuel Smiles. Edward Banks was a navvy engaged upon building a road at Merstham who won promotion to foreman by his industry and sobriety. He educated himself, married the daughter of his former employer and became the builder of London, Southwark and Waterloo bridges before dying a very rich man in 1835. There is a yew tree in this churchyard which is said to be older than the church itself and there is also mention of a thirteenth-century grave slab "outside the vestry window" which we could not find, hard though we searched. There was an old grave-slab outside the *east* window so perhaps this was the one referred to.

This church gains greatly from its setting, for it stands close to a large open space dotted with trees and occasional benches—a sort of village green.

Between the end of the Roman era and the coming of the railway age there was little development of the central chalk plateau. There are remains of the Neolithic hill fort on Banstead Heath and a Roman villa with, perhaps, an attendant temple from which, in 1772, a brass figure of Aesculapius was removed, on Walton Heath. From then onwards, except in one small corner, the hunting laws kept the region empty virtually until the railways stretched out, the Epsom Downs line in 1865 and the Tattenham Corner extension in 1901. Commuterdom had arrived and grass gave place to bricks and mortar; new communities sprang up in a flash with schools, shops and new churches. Kingswood, once a distant chapelry of Ewell, began to house the wealthy, and now, among modern mansions in every conceivable architectural style, only Lovelands Farm and the Old Mint House are relics, albeit much restored, of the sixteenth and seventeenth centuries. Just to the west, Tadworth, inseparable from Burgh Heath, is a labyrinth of suburban streets, with only the splendid eighteenth-century Tadworth Place, now the country branch of a children's hospital, to recall the once spacious past.

Walton-on-the-Hill, with Walton Heath Golf Course as its focal point, is the only one of these villages to preserve something of its history. It was an ancient manor and its name may come from 'weall tun', or walled farmstead. It fell into the possession of Richard de Tonbridge and so of the Clare family, but it came finally into royal control in 1437 because of the drying up of the female succession. In 1465 it was granted to Elizabeth Woodville, Edward IV's wife, "in part support of her expenses of her chamber". In 1509 it was given, by Henry VIII, to Catherine of Aragon and she leased it to the Carew family. It seems that it appeared later as part of Jane Seymour's dowry, and, in the abnormal conditions of the day, it was presented to Anne of Cleves in 1540. When you add to this the fact that in 1539, doubtless because of conscientious opposition to Henry's marital machinations, Sir Nicholas Carew, the leaseholder, was attainted and beheaded for treason, it is clear that Walton played no small part in the troubled history of that period.

There are several old buildings here, much worked over and improved in the course of time. The Old Manor House contains, it seems, some part of the great hall and the chapel of the original Tudor mansion, but it is now uninteresting flats, and in its grounds is an artificial mound that may have been the motte of the Norman castle. Along the street and down Deans Lane are a number of attractive houses, notably Chucks Cottage, Ebenezer Cottage, Yeoman House, Priors, and Walton Hurst.

Not much of the old church, and this not the first one on the site in all probability, is now standing. The first of many rebuildings took place about 1816, when the fabric was found to have been almost destroyed by ivy. Most of the chancel survived that reconstruction, and the tower was added in 1820. In 1868 the north aisle was tacked on. In the chancel are a piscina with shelf and sedilia that date from the thirteenth century and an unusual blocked window fairly low down on the north side. It is not known exactly what purpose this can have served.

In the eastern window of the south side of the nave is a conglomeration of pieces of glass, one, a seated St. Augustine in white and gold, dating from the fifteenth century, and the rest, some good and some very rough, from later periods. It seems that several pieces came from Woburn Abbey; in the 1830s the Duke of Bedford gave these away and the Vicar of Tooting obtained some of the loot; he became Rector of Walton and transferred his booty to the church here.

The oldest fitment in the church is the font, but even this has not come unscathed through the ages. It is believed to be Norman workmanship dating from about 1150, and it may well be the oldest of the twenty-nine lead fonts that exist in the country. Originally, however, it was larger than now, and it is easy to see where it has been, very ham-handedly, reduced to its present size; one of the figures that adorn the sides is half hidden by roughly folded lead. There were once twelve figures, or rather four, three times repeated, of the four Doctors of the Church, Ambrose, Jerome, Gregory the Great, and Augustine of Hippo, seated under semicircular arches. Now there are nine.

The interior of the building is light and well kept, a very pleasant place, and outside the north wall of the chancel is a plain burial slab believed to contain the remains of

"Johannes de Waltune Hujus Ecclesae fundator—A.D. 1268", if you believe the painted notice.

Headley has a fine, high position, a nice old (but much altered) pub, 'The Cock'; Headley Court, which is an R.A.F. rehabilitation centre; and a nineteenth-century church. There was once an old church on this fine site and parts of it, including a font, have been embodied into a curious construction in the churchyard which resembles a grotto. The modern church lacks distinction though the chancel roof is attractive.

Juniper Hall gives Mickleham its chief claim to fame; now a field-study centre, it is an eighteenth-century house (with some fine examples of Adam's work in it) which was built by a certain David Jenkinson who leased it to a group of aristocratic refugees from the French Revolution, including such celebrated personalities as Madame de Staël and the Duc de Montmorency. One of these refugees, General D'Arblay, married Fanny Burney in Mickleham church in 1793 (an occasion suitably commemorated by a plaque in the church). Seventy years later, George Meredith, also a novelist, was married there and then lived on Box Hill. Literary associations are numerous in this area: in Fredley Manor, a delightful sixteenth-century house extremely well restored and dating from 1532, lived Richard Sharp who, though not himself a writer, was a friend of many famous literary men at the end of the eighteenth century and earned himself the nickname of 'Conversation Sharp'; his literary interests did not interfere with the amassing of a handsome fortune which enabled him to offer hospitality as well as good talk to his friends. At the foot of the beautiful wooded road which leads down from Mickleham to join the main Dorking road is the famous Burford Bridge Hotel, built in 1800 but very considerably altered and modernized since—a process still in hand as we write. Here John Keats stayed and finished "Endymion", Nelson slept here for his last night upon English soil before the voyage that ended so gloriously and so tragically at Trafalgar, and Robert Louis Stephenson was a frequent visitor. Few English hotels can boast of such illustrious guests nor indeed of a finer position, for the Burford Bridge nestles at the foot of Box Hill whose green beauty makes a remarkably effective backcloth to the building.

In Mickleham village, note should be taken of another hotel, even older than the 'Burford Bridge'; this is 'The Running Horses', a seventeenth-century building also considerably restored, and near to it is The Old House, built in 1636 with good Dutch gables, and Burmester House, a handsome eighteenth-century residence.

Opposite the 'Running Horses' is St. Michael's Church. Those entering the churchyard from the Dorking side will be greeted at once by a wooden gravestone marking the resting place of one John Walker who died in 1813 and whose inscription runs thus:

Farwell all my Friends so kind
I Hope in Heaven my soul you'll find.

The church is Norman but had its north aisle added in 1872 and, to quote F. R. Banks' Penguin Guide to Surrey, was "severely restored in 1891". 'Severely' seems to us to be an admirable adverb to apply to the well-meaning but often aesthetically disastrous efforts of our Victorian forebears, though the remarkable 'pepperpot' turret at the south-east end of the church cannot be called severe, resembling rather some excessive Byzantine influence at work upon the architect.

Once again, it is a matter of looking for the good things left untouched by the restorers. There are plenty of these in Mickleham church, especially the Norman porch, the tombs inside the porch, and the doorway with its massive wooden door. When Shakespeare put into the mouth of Mercutio the words "tis not so deep as a well nor as wide as a church door" it must have been of just such a portal as this that he was thinking. The two tombs probably date from the years 1330–40 and were originally found opposite the north door. The interior of the church presents an immediate surprise because the chancel is not in line with the nave; this is sometimes known as a 'weeping chancel' because the southward angle of it is supposed to represent Christ's head on the Cross. The nave, chancel and south aisle date from the late twelfth century, as do the handsome lancet windows, but restoration in 1848 made many changes in the church, and the east end in particular is unfortunate in its windows. There is a pleasant pulpit which came from Belgium in 1840 but is presumably much older, a fine Norman font, square and squat, and the Norbury chapel which has an altar tomb with a brass of William Wyddowsoun, citizen and mercer, and Jone, his wyfe; he died in 1514. Ogilvy queries whether the brasses in fact belong to the tomb. The panelling here came from St. Paul's School when it was still located in the cathedral churchyard; it was destroyed in the Great Fire of London in 1666 and this panelling is said to have been salvaged from the blaze.

Some idea of what restoration meant in terms of destruction can be gathered from the following facts: in 1823 a gallery was built (it has since been removed) at the expense of twelfth-century arches and pillars, while the addition of a north aisle meant the destruction of the original north wall in 1872; in the same year, the fine east window was replaced by the present unhappy one.

The reredos dates from 1938 and there are some panelling plaques from Bohemia which are rather oddly covered with a red and white curtain. In the churchyard are six heads in three groups of two along the north wall; these presumably were saved from the restoration.

5

Greensand 1 (East)

UNDER the southern edge of the Downs, in a fairly narrow strip, runs the line of the Folkstone Beds of the Lower Greensand. These beds are the most fertile type of the several soils known collectively as greensand which further west may come out as a coarse gravelly base through which the water runs easily, extracting all the useful minerals and so creating tracts of unfertile heathland. The Folkstone Beds cling close to the chalk throughout the length of the country. Our earliest ancestors were quick to appreciate their fertility, and some of the Neolithic and Iron Age settlements come into being along what came to be called the Vale of Holmesdale.

The A25, notorious for its bottlenecks, runs along this vale, slicing through villages and thundering down ancient high streets. A new motorway now being constructed along the edge of the Downs will, doubtless, serve to restore these old places to their ancient peace. We follow the vale from the eastern border of the county through to Dorking in this chapter.

In 1934 Frederick Delius died in the French village in which he had spent much of his life and was buried there. But he had often expressed a wish to be buried in an English village and in 1935 his body was moved to the churchyard at Limpsfield where it rests today. Limpsfield church is a fine one, which retains some original parts, notably the tower of the late twelfth century. The tower is shingled and low but possesses an impressive strength. Inside, there is clear evidence of the restoration in 1871–2 when much of the east wall was rebuilt and an organ (not the present one) was put in. Five years after this restoration two new bells were added to the four already *in situ*, one of which dates from the late fourteenth century and another from 1619.

Despite the restoration, St. Peter's is still a very beautiful and interesting church: the north chapel, called the Gresham chapel, is thirteenth century, as are the south arcade and aisle. When the Gresham chapel was built, Limpsfield church came under the control of the Abbey of Battle which appointed the rector, though allowing him to retain the revenues. It may have been an Abbot of Battle who ordered the construction of this chapel, in which part of a blocked doorway near the east end and the fifteenth-century window in the north wall should be noted. The Gresham family obtained the manor of Limpsfield when Battle Abbey was dissolved in the reign of Henry VIII and they retained it until 1742; it then changed hands several times until another Gresham regained it for the family; this man's granddaughter married into the Leveson-Gower family who still occupy a prominent position in the affairs of this district.

In the chancel can be seen an oven for the baking of Communion wafers, one of only five surviving in Surrey. This is behind the present Communion table, close to another recess which would appear to have been once used to house a sacred relic. So that the baking of the wafers could be properly supervised, there was a low window at the east end of the south wall so placed as to throw light upon the oven recess. In the south wall is a piscina, a sedile, and a third recess with a segmental head whose former purpose remains uncertain.

In the nave there was once, at the west end, a fifteenth-century window, unhappily replaced in the first half of the nineteenth century—some years before the main restoration was carried out, in the course of which the west gallery was removed. The north aisle was added in 1851; the south arcade, however, dates from the early thirteenth century when that aisle was constructed.

Limpsfield itself has a number of delightful old houses in its main street, one of them being a bookshop. Middle Cottage, April Cottage, Court Cottage and Palmer's are all noteworthy and so is the large, partly half-timbered Detillens House and the attractive row of cottages which take their name from this house. The rectory, opposite the church, is Georgian and to the south of the church is the manor house where Eugenia Stanhope once lived: she was the wife of Lord Chesterfield's son and she published her father-in-law's famous letter to her husband.

One historical situation that constantly crops up in these villages along the greensand belt under the Downs is the gradual assumption of the lordship of the manor by wealthy citizens of London, a situation that has by no means finished even now. It may be that the old Roman roads still in Elizabeth's reign provided a sure carriageway to that part of the county. Certainly both Limpsfield and Oxted found rich new merchant lords in that century of commercial enterprise.

Oxted, mentioned briefly in Domesday as having a church, was called 'Ac Stede', or the place of oak trees. It came under the sway of the Cobhams of Starborough Castle and changed hands frequently when that family lost its biological drive until, in 1587, it came into the hands of Charles Hoskins, a merchant of London. The male line of that family, even, died out within 200 years. By 1798, indeed, the inheritance had to pass to an aunt.

The manor house of Oxted, Barrow Green House, has some rather more recent historical connections that stand in opposition to the normal conservative preoccupations of that neighbourhood. About the beginning of the last century Jeremy Bentham, the radical political thinker, was living in the house. Perhaps it was the sight of the activities in the local 'rotten boroughs' of Blechingley and Gatton that inspired some of his principal tenets: that voting should be secret and that M.P.s should be paid. He must be regarded as one of the chief architects of the Reform Bill of 1832.

Barrow Green Court still stands, and behind more recent façades is a seventeenth-century building. The farm is older. This was not always the manor house. That was Oxted Court, and it seems to have been Charles Hoskins who settled in the other house. The manor was held, before the Conquest, by Gida, Harold's mother. William awarded it to count Eustace of Boulogne. It was held from him by a family which took its name from the place, and there is a record of one Roland de Oxted claiming, in 1278, the prescriptive liberties of "view of frankpledge, assize of bread and ale, pillory,

tumbril, gallows, infangenthef, outfangenthef, waif, ancient warren in his demesne land, and an ancient park from time beyond
memory". The jury, we are pleased to recall, upheld his claim as
being true "from time beyond memory".

The village seems to have grown up in two sections. Old Oxted
stretches along the narrow High Street along which now pours the
A25. As it descends the hill this High Street has formed a cutting,
possibly—as with a number of sunken lanes and roads in the
Greensand districts—as a result of traffic and of weather. This situation has led to a number of the old cottages having steps down
from the front door to the road level. There are several delightful
old cottages, mainly sixteenth and seventeenth century, as well
as three hostelries of the same periods, the 'Bell' which juts out
into the street and overhangs at one point, the 'Crown' in which
the later refronting can easily be seen, and the 'George'. They, at
least, have owed their prosperity to that ancient highway that is
now the A25.

The old church, as well as the other section of the village,
stands nearly a mile to the north-east, beside a wide expanse of
green with a pleasant cricket ground, and not far from the railway. Although there are some old houses here, too, the proximity
of the station has led inevitably to a great build-up of commuter
dwellings. Most of these are on the other side of the line, and
there they almost link up with Limpsfield. At least one old barn
there has been skilfully adapted to modern requirements by forming the basis of the Barn Theatre.

The church has had a disastrous history; it has been struck
and severely damaged by lightning, in 1637 and in 1719, and then,
after repairs and rebuilding at those times, it was ruthlessly restored in 1877. That cannot be the whole story of reconstruction
work either, judging by the curious hotch-potch of styles to be
found. The great squat tower is Norman, a massive amalgam of
stone and rubble and mortar held together by mighty stone quoins.
Beside it the nave looks very tall. The south doorway is fourteenth-
century work and the door itself is probably contemporary with it.
The porch dates from about 100 years later and it contains the
remains of a holy-water stoup. The aisles were added in the fourteenth century and the arcade pillars in the fifteenth.

The chancel is slightly offset from the line of the nave and appears to have been built not long before the time of the first recorded rector, Adam de Stratton, who died in 1294, although the east window's fine curvilinear tracery is somewhat later. Above its modern glass there are four remnants of the original fourteenth-century glass, where the four evangelists are represented by their symbols and their names are given in Lombardic capitals as Johan, Marc, Lucas and Matheus. In the south wall is a piscina and shelf and, behind some panelling, the top just visible, a priest's door. In the wall to the north of the altar is an arched cavity, possibly for a tomb that has disappeared or for an Easter sepulchre. Leading from the north chapel is an unusual passageway to the chancel. Its purpose is conjectural, but it may have been a sort of enlarged squint. The doorway to the staircase leading to the old rood loft can be seen on the south side of the chancel arch, and some relics of wall painting seem still to exist at the sides of the chancel arch facing the nave.

In the chancel there are several brasses, the oldest of the fifteenth century, and another at the side whose lettering we could not decipher but which may be that to "Johes Page quondam Rector hujus Ecclie", of 1428. On the north wall is the excellent memorial to John Aldersey, haberdasher and merchant, and to his wife Anna, who after forty-six years "in y holy Aestate of matrimony . . . had ysue 17 children"; all are represented below the parents.

Apart from these, almost all the memorials commemorate members of the Hoskins family, one slab bearing the curious wording:

Let this
Patterne of Piety
Mapp of Misery
Mirrour of Patience
Here rest.

Above it, on the wall, is another on which the person about whom the eulogy is written is not named, but who is commemorated by what must bid fair to be some of the worst verse ever written. As short quotation will demonstrate this perhaps:

... In her affliction dolorous and many,
Her patience scarcely paralleld by any;
Of perfect happiness she could not miss
Led by such graces to eternall blisse.

The search for 'eternall blisse' perhaps inspired the canons of
Tandridge Priory, an offshoot of Southwark that stood, before
the Dissolution, a little to the south. Tandridge is something of
a mystery. Even its name defeats the philologists. But that is not
all; at one time it dominated the countryside and a plaque beside
the A25 records the fact that one of the earliest of local Parlia-
ments held their deliberations near that spot close to a noble
eighteenth-century house formerly called Rooks Nest. Now the
Hundred bears the name of Tandridge. The Priory of the Augustin-
ians must have been a powerful establishment; neither Newark nor
Chertsey achieved such posthumous fame.

In the churchyard is an immensely old yew, still a magnificent
tree. Apparently there was once a Saxon church here and its foundations were laid to avoid this self-same tree, which gives some in-
dication of its age. The present church has a small Norman priest's
door and a tiny window of the same age on the north side of the
chancel. Apart from these and the sturdy early thirteenth-century
timber of the spire, the existing fabric is almost entirely a rebuilding by Gilbert Scott. The village itself is rather uninteresting.

The geographical position of Godstone is not a particularly
happy one for a village since the A22 and the A25 meet here; as
both of these are extremely busy, especially in the summer, it is
remarkable that the village has managed to preserve so much that
is attractive.

In Saxon times there was a settlement here called 'Walcnes-
tead' which later developed into 'Walkingstede'. 'Walking' here
means fulling and the dictionary definition of fulling is 'scouring
and beating as a means of finishing or cleansing woollens' so that
Walkingstede is 'the place where woollen cloth is finally processed'.
There may also have been a Saxon village named 'God's tun' or
'Guda's tun', Guda being the daughter of Edward the Confessor.
She married Eustace of Boulogne who was given Walkingstead.

The focal point of modern Godstone is the village green, complete with cricket pitch and a small pond; the church however, does

not here form part of the surroundings of the green, for it stands in near-isolation about half a mile from the green and is reached either by turning left up Church Lane or, more pleasantly for the traveller on foot, by a lane which starts near 'The White Hart', the magnificent public-house-cum-restaurant which is one of the most striking buildings in the area.

This was reputedly built in the time of Richard II whose badge was a white hart, but there is no evidence in the building of today of construction earlier than the middle of the sixteenth century. The name was changed from 'The White Hart' to the 'Clayton Arms' at the request of a certain Sir Robert Clayton but reverted to its former title quite recently. The inn figures in legend and in literature: it was a famous coaching inn and is supposed to have provided a resting-place for the Czar of Russia and other notables in 1815 when they were *en route* to a boxing match at Blindley-heath.

Some internal restoration and alteration has clearly taken place but a plethora of genuine beams, of massive wooden doors and of sudden unexpected steps bears witness to its antiquity. On the opposite side of the main road and a little to the south of 'The White Hart' is 'The Bell', a pleasant two-storeyed inn of the eighteenth century. As Godstone also has the 'Fox and Hounds', part of which is of the seventeenth century and 'The White Swan' of the eighteenth century, neither visitors nor locals can complain that they are compelled to take their refreshments in surroundings of revolting modernity.

It was in the reign of Elizabeth I that the church acquired its present comparative isolation when the Roman road, unused for centuries, was restored to service and the villagers moved their cottages to be closer to it. The medieval church survived this desertion but fell, most unfortunately, into the hands of Victorian restorers who went about their work so thoroughly as to destroy virtually every trace of its former glories. Sir Gilbert Scott was the architect responsible for this restoration and for the south chancel aisle and, though his reconstruction was in the style of the four-teenth century, his work will hardly delight those who prefer originals to copies. A window in the west wall and a blocked-in doorway near to it are both of the thirteenth century and the font

A rural scene near Waverley Abbey

Hill House Farm, Thursley

(above) Mill House, Elstead

(below) The barn at Peper Harow

Leigh Church

The priest's house at Leigh

Detail of the chancel screen at Charlwood Church

is two centuries later but otherwise everything is Sir Gilbert except for some monuments and memorial brasses of the seventeenth century; most of these relate to the Evelyn family, one of whom, Sir John, has a good marble altar-tomb dating from 1664. This is of interest because it was constructed while Sir John was still alive; he is shown in plate armour and his wife Thomasin in a loose robe. Sir John outlived his wife and children and left his estate to Mary Gittings, euphemistically described in a book published in 1902 as "the lady of his affections".

The almshouses next to the church were built by Sir Gilbert in a not unattractive mock-Tudor style; attached to the eight dwellings is a chapel also designed by Scott with happier results than attended his efforts in the church.

Church Lane runs past the church; it is narrow and winding and contains three splendid old houses, largest and finest of which is called the Old Pack House (a further reference to the wool industry in this title) which was apparently an inn at one time and is still listed as one in a book published only fifteen years ago.

Just past the Old Pack House, Church Lane forms a T-junction with the A22 and a turn right into it will bring the visitor back into the village. Around this are houses of very many different periods, almost a miniature history of English domestic architecture and yet forming a most harmonious and attractive whole; those on the southern side would appear to be the oldest, while to the west are one or two large mid-Victorian houses which have a dignity and style characteristic of their period and which recall the leisured society of that time.

It seems likely that the new motorway, running cross the county from Egham to the Kent border north of Westerham, will take away much traffic from Godstone. Thus Godstone will to some extent recapture the tranquility of the days when it was a prominent place in the important leather industry of Surrey or when Evelyn briefly established his gunpowder works there. It may be that the new motorway will save Godstone, as well as Blechingley and Oxted from the fate of becoming a 'swamped' village.

A25 is not the easiest of roads; on its often narrow and tortuous progress eastwards into Kent it passes through a number of

G

splendid villages to whose peace and quiet it makes no contribution. One of the best of these villages is Blechingley or Bletchingley as it is often spelt. This has a marvellous church and a lovely main street, lovely, that is, except for one appalling eyesore. On the north side before the church is reached, there was once a house called Hall House. In 1860 this gave way to almshouses and these in turn, in 1965, to something to which politeness alone prevents us from giving a name. So utterly out of keeping with its neighbours, with the houses opposite, and indeed with the entire village, is this edifice that we were surprised to find that a plaque upon it makes no attempt to conceal its perpetrators to whom we at least will grant anonymity.

This apart, there is much to admire. 'The Whyte Harte' dates from 1388 and has been an inn since that time, a record which few inns in England can equal. Blechingley village is even older, for the manor was granted by William the Conqueror to Richard de Tonbridge and it was very probably his son who built the castle, of which nothing now remains; the site alone can be seen in the grounds of a private house in a lane to the south of the High Street. For nearly 200 years, from 1347 until 1521, the Staffords held the manor but in the latter year Edward, Duke of Buckingham, was charged with plotting against Henry VIII (using his Blechingley palace to do so) and was executed. Buckingham had foolishly boasted of the royal blood in his veins and had also shown too clearly his contempt for Henry's low-born minister, Cardinal Wolsey.

After Buckingham's death, the manor passed to Sir Nicholas Carew but he was no more fortunate than his predecessor, being himself executed. Anne of Cleves' short-lived marriage to the uxorious king had for her a happier ending for she was given Blechingley Palace as her place of comfortable retirement; when she died, she bequeathed it to her steward, Sir Thomas Cawarden, who had formerly been Keeper of the Tents, Toyles and Hayles and Master of the Revels to the King. He kept a hundred liveried servants when he was the proud owner of the palace. Cawarden's lavish tomb in Blechingley church chronicles, with disarming simplicity, the convolutions of his career: an ardent reformer under Edward VI, he became an equally ardent Catholic under

Mary Tudor and, presumably, an ardent Anglican under Elizabeth! His date of death is variously given as 1559 and 1561.

Sir Thomas has taken us a long way from 'The Whyte Harte' and the village. Blechingley, small though it was, returned two M.P.s to the Commons in the days before Parliamentary reform did away with such 'rotten' boroughs; from 1733 onwards, the election (if it can be rightly so called!) took place in 'The Whyte Harte', where no doubt free beer helped the tiny handful of voters to make a wise choice. The last member returned by Blechingley before the Reform Bill of 1832 deprived it of its representation was none other than the future Lord Palmerston, later a Foreign Minister and Prime Minister of well-deserved reputation.

On the same side of the High Street as this inn can be seen some attractive cottages notably those called, quaintly, 'The Cobbles' and Melrose Cottage. On the opposite side, King Charles' House (formerly the Market House), the post office and its cottage and the eighteenth-century Norfolk House are all excellent, as is the sixteenth-century (restored) Clerk's House. Further east is The Plough Inn, which is seventeenth-century and also restored, and in Outwood Lane a third admirable hostelry should be noted, the sixteenth-century Prince Albert. In the area known as Pendell, to the north of the High Street, there is the handsome Pendell Court (1624 with considerable additions in the late nineteenth century), Pendell Farm and Pendell House (1636) with an outstanding garden. In Little Common Lane there is The Old Cottage and not far away is Cockley Cottage which was once the village pest house. To the south of the village is the oddly named Rabies Heath district with one outstanding cottage turned into a delightful house and called the 'Brick Kiln', a name which implies that brick-making was once carried out in this district.

Before visiting the church, note the fine cottages of Church Walk: the Nicholas Wolmer Cottage of 1552 (restored), Nos. 1 to 5, and Legg's Cottages (seventeenth-century restored); behind these can be seen the fine barn and stables of Selmes Farm. Church Walk was once the High Street of the village, which, according to Aubrey, then had seven churches, improbable as it may sound.

The one church that is very definitely still in existence is fine; it is also one of the best-kept churches that we have seen in our

travels round Surrey; in particular, the various and numerous interesting points in it are extremely well and clearly labelled, so
making a detailed account here quite superfluous. The structure
itself, however, demands some attention. The tower was built
about 1090 and heightened about seventy years later; the crenella-
tion at its summit is modern and the absence of a spire is accounted
for by the fact that the one that was there was destroyed by
lightning in 1606, the resultant fire also destroying the fine peal
of bells.

One of the most interesting things about this church is that
the really major changes in it were made in 1460 rather than in
the Victorian restoration over 400 years later. In 1460 the chap-
lain to the Duke of Buckingham was Hugh Hextall and he seems
to have been very active in the service of Blechingley church. A
perpendicular-style window thus replaced the original Early English lancets and was itself replaced in 1870 by the present three
lancets when the architect Butterfield carried out the restoration.
In 1460 the south aisle and the south chapel were very greatly
altered. It is thought that the south chapel once contained the
cell of the local hermit, Brother Roger, who was granted a bushel
of wheat by Henry III in 1233 and who may have been one of the
first Franciscans to live in England. The massive south door and
the porch date from 1460 and over the porch is still the room
which was used for storing military supplies during Elizabeth
I's reign.

Reference has already been made to the monument to Sir
Thomas Cawarden. Even more dominating than this is the one to
Sir Robert Clayton's wife. Sir Robert was Lord Mayor of London
in 1679–80 and was mentioned (not favourably) in the second
part of the great satirical poem *Absolom and Achitophel*:

> Ishban, of conscience suited to his trade,
> As good a saint as usurer ever made.

The implication here is that Sir Robert was as willing to change
his political alliances as Sir Thomas Cawarden has been to change
his religious loyalties. The Clayton memorial is by Richard
Crutcher and has been described by a writer on Blechingley earlier
in this century as "like a fearful nightmare".

Cobbett called Blechingley a "vile, rotten Borough" but clearly allowed his detestation of corrupt politics to get the better of him. In his time, as now, Blechingley had many attractions.

Hidden away from the traffic a little to the north of Blechingley is the scatter of cottages called Brewer Street. There is a fine fifteenth-century half-timbered farmhouse, relatively unrestored, there, called by the same name, a perfect example of the smaller Tudor mansion.

Like an iceberg, Buckland shows only the tip, the village green with its pond and ecclesiastical barn that appears in the photographs, and the little church on the other side of the A25 that the experts disregard. Given a fair measure of luck, Buckland thinks, that will do the trick and the world in its car will hurry by. It shows modern little houses down the road towards Betchworth to deceive the unsuspecting travellers.

Even in Norman days Buckland kept itself tucked away and out of sight. It went, with the rest of the spoils, to Richard de Tonbridge and followed the same history as the other Clare possessions. It early came, however, under William the Conqueror's forestry rules and limitations which bound lord as well as commoner. To hold the manor of Buckland, therefore, was not to have the right to exploit the land; that right had already gone to the king. It was not until 1268 that John de Wauton who then held the manor in sub-fee was granted the right of free warren, which allowed him to hunt here freely on the land which he had obtained.

The very name of Buckland shows its connection with the preservation of game. Another manor here was called Hartswood, so it is clear that the whole area was from early days given over to the red deer. The old primitive west-east track on the chalk slopes passed only a little way to the north and it is believed that there was an ancient inn, used by travellers, in the parish. This, later called the 'Harvesters', still exists as a building, though not as an inn, up Lawrence Lane, the present structure dating, it is believed, from about 1500.

The village green is attractive and has, apart from Street Farm with its fine black barn of the seventeenth century on the west side, three tiny cottages of the sixteenth century, formerly the 'Brew House', on the eastern flank. If you go down Rectory Lane, which heads northwards to the Downs from here, you will pass several picturesque cottages, the tile-hung Oak Cottage, much of which is of the seventeenth century, and the newly prettified 'Stonecrop' until you come to the railway.

This is another world and another age. Beyond the railway the lane soon peters out as you come to Old Kemp's Farm, another of those splendid, stalwart massed buildings that have clearly been added to and rebuilt at various times in history. The view along the chalk escarpment to Betchworth clump with the chalk quarries standing out against the ripe barley is superb. Don't invade it with the car. To do so would mean that you would have to "RING FOR GATEKEEPER", as the sign on the gate says. Another notice beside the line warns against trespassing, headed:

"SOUTH EASTERN & CHATHAM RAILWAY
MANAGEMENT COMMITTEE".

The gatekeeper lives in a tiny cottage built in railway mock-Gothick, and his wife, one fine afternoon, entertained me at length with her experiences and her views on modern life. It was all a most pleasant occasion, set as it was against the lovely blackcloth of the Downs.

There has long been a church here. In 1725 the rector was able to report to his bishop that "here was no chapel, no lecturer, no curate, no Papist, no Non-conformists, no school". In 1860 the church was rebuilt almost completely with only the timber belfry being retained almost as it had been before. This is not to say that the building lacks interest or attraction. The window opposite the door has had some old glass of about 1380 fitted into it. This contains the figures of Saints Peter and Paul, their heads apparently being a little later in date than the bodies and some of the surrounds. A little further along in another window in the north wall is a delicate little Virgin and Child of the fifteenth century done in a method known as 'silver stain'. The east window was put up after the last war as a memorial, the previous Victorian glass having been destroyed by enemy action. The whole east end is, in fact, a credit to the parish; there is a pleasant reredos of a tendril and leaf motif in pale gold on a cool, pale blue background, and the modern frontal in deep green with an abstract flower design in

gilt and shades of russet sets it off perfectly. The place is beautifully cared for and quite admirable in its simplicity.

At the time of Edward the Confessor, the manor of East Betchworth, or Becci's Farm, was held by a thegn with the remarkable
name of Cola. Surely some enterprising advertising agent could
make use of him! After the Conquest the manor went to Richard
de Tonbridge. Around 1088 it came into the hands of William
de Warenne, the first Earl of Surrey, and thence to the Earl of
Arundel in 1361. That part of its history it has in common with
many others of our villages. Gradually, as elsewhere, the estates
became parcelled out among other owners and there remains little
of interest to be found in history. Even the castle simply crumbled
away and seems never to have seen a shot fired in anger. What remains of it lies by the river in Betchworth Golf Course, over beyond Brockham which was separated from Betchworth only in
1848.

The origin of the name shows that the community was established as an agricultural unit. It lies principally on the Lower
Greensand where the Mole makes it into excellent growing soil,
and the early settlement, as usual, ran up on to the chalk and down
into the forest. Brockham parish, being new, is only a lump carved
out of its north-west corner and does not have such an extension;
nor does Buckland, which, although an old independent manor,
was solely concerned with hunting. The heart of old Betchworth,
naturally enough, is to be found beside the river. The last hundred
years has seen the place spread up towards the A25 road until it
is almost linked with Buckland, and much of the new building has
been in more or less happy approximations to the styles of past
ages.

Betchworth Place, the big house, stands at the head of a wide
southward meander of the Mole, just near where the bridge spans
the river, where a crossing must for centuries have existed. The
house was built in 1625, but it was extended and somewhat refurbished in the eighteenth century. Against its northern wall
stands the church in its large and tree-surrounded yard.

Before 1850 this church must have been far more interesting
than it is now. Presumably it had fallen into considerable dis-
repair; why else should it have undergone such a massive recon-

struction? The whole tower then standing over the crossing between nave and chancel was moved bodily to its present position on the southern side at the end of the south aisle. A small Norman arch that had been on the western side of the tower was then rebuilt and forms the east end of the south aisle where the tower begins. Part of a Saxon pillar was inserted beside the modern window at the south side of the tower, evidence at least of the antiquity of the original building that had been refashioned, in fact, early in the thirteenth century, when the aisles had been built and the rough openings for the uncommon clerestory of the nave had been cut. The three lancets on the north side of the chancel as well as the nave arcades all date from the same period. Just inside the door, in the south wall, is an old holy water stoup, perhaps of the fourteenth century. On the other side of the door is a modern font, designed as a memorial by Eric Kennington. It is doubtless heresy to criticize this, but it does look rather like a vast egg-cup.

There are other, older, memorials elsewhere, notably a fine brass portrait of a priest in Mass vestments, holding a chalice. This is for William Wardysworth, vicar of the parish, who died in 1533. On the south wall of the Lady Chapel are some small brass plates, the oldest being inscribed to Thomas Morsted and his wife Alianora. It was placed there by their son, also Thomas Morsted, surgeon to Henry V at the Battle of Agincourt in 1415. He became High Sheriff of London before his death in 1450. The other two are both from the seventeenth century.

In Church Road, forming a little square outside the church are some attractive buildings, cottages of the seventeenth century, some tumbledown barns, and the old vicarage of 1715. These make a picturesque group, while in the main street beyond, leading down to the river, are several others, Old House, a long and remarkably thin Queen Anne residence, the Dolphin Inn, probably basically of the fifteenth or sixteenth century, facing various ancient cottages clustered round the entrance to the park. Up beyond the bridge leading up to Snowerhill Farm is a pair of half-timbered farm cottages that have not, up to now, been too much doctored.

If you turn down the road that leads off westwards just below the Dolphin Inn, you will soon come to Wonham Manor House.

This has half-timbered gables, a great chimney made of hard chalk, or clunch, which has the weatherbeaten head of what looks like a Bishop let into it, a garden wall where the bricks have been laid above an earlier wall, again of clunch, and a line of three cottages that look like a film set, and in whose garden we saw a magnificent blue macaw when we passed one day. The experts tell us that Wonham is of the seventeenth century with later additions. We would have thought it a little earlier than that, Elizabethan certainly, but then that lady did last into the seventeenth century.

"There are very few prettier rides in England and the weather was beautifully fine. There are more meeting-places than churches in the vale and I have heard of no less than five people, in this vale, who have gone crazy on account of religion."

Thus William Cobbett describing a journey made on 21st October 1825 through Buckland, Betchworth, Dorking, Shere and Albury. His comments on the spread of non-conformity in this part of Surrey are interesting as is the assertion that madness had overtaken some of its more ardent followers. Nowadays, it is doubtful whether any of the people who live in this delightful vale will be driven out of their wits by the violence of their theological passions.

Brockham Green possesses one of the most-photographed village cricket grounds in England, let alone in Surrey. When the church was built in 1847 the architect, Benjamin Ferrey, sited it most splendidly at the south end of the green which was already an attractive place because of the old houses, particularly on its north and east sides. Today, the green is the property of the local council and there is some talk of asking the cricket club to transfer its matches to the new recreation ground south of the green; the trouble is that watching cricket in such an ideal setting has become very popular with people in cars and there is a fear that, sooner or later, a well-struck ball will cause some serious damage, for the green is small and a village Jessop would play havoc with the cars outside the boundaries. It would be a great pity if cricket ceased to be played on this marvellous site for it has seen many of the great players in action, including W. G. Grace.

On Guy Fawkes' Night, the green is the scene of a vast bonfire and a fireworks display; this used to be a pleasant, local celebration but in recent years it has attracted some 'foreigners' whose respect for the residents' property is not always conspicuous.

There was once a duck-pond where the church now stands and its absence from the green is to be regretted since a little water invariably enhances the attraction of the village. However, it is not long ago since Brockham Green won the annual competition for the best-kept, large village in Surrey and a visit to it in 1970 suggested that it would not be long before this honour again came its way.

The church was built of clunch, and this has needed considerable refacing in the last twenty years. The money for this expensive task has been raised by the parishioners: Brockham Green is fortunate in possessing a large number of loyal residents who are determined to maintain the village and its buildings. Another characteristic of Brockham Green is its love of music attested by the excellence of the local choir which usually makes a fine showing at the annual Leith Hill festival.

There is nothing remarkable about the interior of the church and it inevitably lacks fittings and furnishings of any antiquity; but, since it is an early Victorian building, it could certainly be a great deal worse than it is. Its proportions are handsome, it has height and spaciousness, and it is impeccably kept.

Of the old houses in the village, perhaps the most interesting is Court Farm, once used by the Dukes of Norfolk as a place in which to break the journey—at that time long and difficult—from London to Arundel. This is a very handsome eighteenth-century house, very much larger than its use as an overnight stopping place would suggest. Much older, and nearer the centre of the village, are Dell's Cottage, 'Dell' being possibly a corruption of 'well', the Vicarage Cottage and the delightful pair of cottages in Wheeler's Lane listed in *Antiquities of Surrey* as numbers sixty-four and sixty-five and ascribed there to the sixteenth century. Note also the fine old bridge crossed by traffic just before reaching the village from the turning off the main road—and at the same time (if such a feat is possible!) close the eyes to the modern pedestrian bridge erected by its side.

In 1972 Brockham Green's Triennial Festival and Fair will be due again and perhaps this most attractive village will celebrate the event by once again winning the best-kept village award; let us hope, moreover, that the cricketers will still be playing in that marvellous setting.

Brockham brings us once again into commuter country close to the good rail service of Dorking itself, a lovely old town set, from ancient times, at the southern end of the Mole Gap and a staging post, no doubt, on the Roman Stane Street.

6

Greensand 2 (Central)

WESTWARDS from Dorking the fertile Folkestone Beds, here fed by the Tillingbourne, still stretch in a line under the lee of the Downs, forming a strip of good farming country early settled by the Bronze and Iron Age people. Remains of round burial barrows have been found in this valley, while just above it, at Abinger, exists what must be one of the earliest of human habitations in the country. This is in the grounds of Abinger Manor House.

As the ice ages gradually receded, man returned to England across the land bridge that still existed. These greensand heights provided the best location for his survival, but, there being no natural caves, he was forced to construct his own shelter. His answer to this problem was not unlike the Eskimo's; he hollowed out a hole in the ground for maximum warmth and covered this hollow with a roof of skins or branches and bracken. A hearth or fire-hole was made outside this shelter. All this took place about 4,000 B.C.

The mesolithic pit-dwelling at Abinger was excavated only in 1950. It was a matter of rare good fortune that the land was then owned by Sir Edward Beddington Behrens. As his land was ploughed it was noted that a large number of flints were being turned up. Sir Edward noted the exact positions of these and called in one of our greatest archaeological experts, Dr. L. S. B. Leakey, who undertook the direction of the excavations, which may be the most valuable mesolithic remains in Europe.

The pit is now housed in a small hut and the ground has been chemically hardened. What can be seen is an irregularly shaped, longish, narrowish hollow, deeper at the far end, towards the west, where the entrance was. Here, on each side, are the holes made for two posts which supported the roof. Beyond these at ground level is the fire-hole.

Vast numbers of flint instruments, chips that were used for splitting and shaping other, bigger implements, as well as rough chisels (burins), axe-heads and even later arrow-heads were found in and around the pit. This has led to the belief that here was the centre of a flint industry, and that this pit was only one of a whole community. Flint is not found naturally in the neighbourhood. It must have been brought, carried on human backs, from the chalk hills, perhaps from Ranmore, to be worked here. Why here? The answer lies, almost certainly, in the good dry, easily hollowed greensand and in the fact that there are two excellent springs. Other flint remains have been found in fair quantities near two pools fed by these two springs.

Another relic of pre-Roman Britain is to be found some 2 miles away to the south, on the top of Holmbury Hill. Here on this high spot, 857 feet above sea level, the Neolithic inhabitants built one of the fortresses that line these heights. The two ditches that once had a stockade between them can still be seen surrounding all but the steep south-facing slope, which was itself terraced below the top and the lower face thereby made more sheer. Some excavation of the camp area his brought to light fragments of pottery and corn-grinding querns. There was a meagre water supply on the east side of the camp itself and a more plentiful source somewhat further down the hill.

Of Roman occupation nothing now remains, though a small villa was found in 1877 in a field near Abinger Place, to the north. The floors and remains were not fortunate in their discoverers. They appear to have been used only by Charles Darwin for researches into the activities of earth-worms. It is hard to believe that this represents the only Roman settlement in this fertile district obviously well known to earlier settlers. Doubtless other relics have been ploughed up in the course of time or are still lying under the soil awaiting discovery.

At the northern end of the parish, too, are found the relics of the other industries that Abinger has, in course of time, fathered. Both are, or were, at Abinger Hammer, a dribble of houses and cottages now, lying along the A25, with a famous inn whose sign is a clock struck at the hours by a hammer-swinging ironman. Medieval iron-working needed water-power to work the forges and the drop-hammers that shaped the pigs of crude iron. Here the Tillingbourne was dammed to yield power and the industry flourished until the North-Country domination took away the trade in the seventeenth century. Today the trade of the Hammer is that of growing cress for Covent Garden. And so the cress beds, the proud hour-striker, and a few ancient cottages are all that remain of what was probably a prosperous community, though it is here that you can see a mandrake, a pansy called an Irish Moll and a plant that smells of milk chocolate in the garden of Dr. and Mrs. Rees-Thomas's lovely house called High Hackhurst. On two days in each year the house and its superb garden are open to the public in aid of a nurses' charity. For ardent horticulturists a visit to the latter must surely be a matter of top priority—and it is the work solely of the doctor and his wife and one full-time gardener!

High Hackhurst itself is a fifteenth-century house, much reconstructed and restored. Until comparatively recently it provided a home for three farm labourers and their families and contained three ladder-type staircases. Soon after the beginning of this century, it passed into the hands of one owner who naturally had to carry out considerable changes in it. He put in the windows which have transformed the large cupboards in the sitting-room into attractive recesses; in 1925 the present fireplace was constructed and so well and tastefully that it fits admirably into the fine oak panelling of late-Tudor origin which flanks it on both sides.

The old house had a large central fireplace which is now in the dining-room which also has some truly magnificent old panelling of an antiquity, it is thought, practically without parallel in any English house. The sitting-room contains an original De Wint and four Wedgwood cameos which add to its attraction very considerably.

The kitchen is spacious, and under the house there is a vast cellar, the existence of which makes it quite clear that High Hackhurst has always been one house and not two or three cottages knocked into one dwelling. It has five good-sized bedrooms, the ceilings of which have been raised. There is a profusion of good beams and of black-and-white timbered walls upstairs though no panelling to equal the antique beauty of that found in the main downstairs rooms.

Delightful though the house is, most visitors will no doubt recall chiefly the garden; it is to be hoped that no future visitor will try to disprove the ancient legend that says that a mandrake screams when it is pulled from the ground!

Abinger parish is long and thin like a church steeple; it is 9 miles in length but never more than one mile in breadth. The common lies plumb in the middle, between the 'Hammer' and the 'Bottom'; it boasts a good inn-restaurant, part of which at least is old, the 'Abinger Hatch', opposite which is the small but pleasant green and St. James' church. On the green are a set of stocks, surrounded unfortunately by ugly iron railings. On the green is held the medieval fair on the second Saturday of every June; this dates from a genuine medieval fair held in the days when the adjacent church was a favourite stopping place for pilgrims. Towards the end of the last century, the Salvation Army made a determined effort on one occasion to prevent the fair being held presumably for the same reasons that prompted the Puritans of the seventeenth century to cut down maypoles and impose a shut-down upon various rural junketings.

Near the church is the manor house built originally by Sir John Evelyn in the 1680s, but very extensively restored partly because of a fire which destroyed one end of it early in the nineteenth century. Today, the hall floor and some of the woodwork is thought to be genuinely old, and the late Jacobean porch, in which intrusive birds annually make their nests, is a fine example of craftsmanship which makes us regret all the more that the original house has not been preserved. In the manor cottage next to it, Max Beerbohm lived during the last war. The manor house was used as a dower house by the Evelyns until 1906; it is now the property of Mr. and Mrs. R. A. Clarke who have furnished its spacious rooms with beautiful furniture and excellent paintings.

Abinger Manor House is unique in one respect for it is certainly the only private house in England (or no doubt in the world) to have a Norman motte in the garden and prehistoric pit-dwellings in a nearby field.

The motte originally had a moat, part of which has been drained in recent times to display the drawbridge supports. Now delightfully covered by trees and daffodils, the motte also has some anemones which recall the ancient saying: "Where blood has been shed or Roman foot has trod, anemones grow". That blood was shed can hardly be doubted for the site was twice fortified, once in 1077 and again between 1135 and 1154—those nineteen long winters "when God and his saints slept" as the barons took advantage of the civil strife waging between Stephen and Matilda, rivals for the English throne. There is a suggestion that the refortification was carried out by a supporter of Matilda, but it is equally possible that its owner may have been merely interested in using it to terrorize the surrounding countryside, for the top of the motte commands a view which must have been even more extensive when it was crowned by the usual central tower of two or even three storeys. Visible today are the markings of the pillars and posts and these show clearly that there must have been a rebuilding of the tower, since there are two sets of post-marks very close to each other.

The castle came into the hands of the Jarpenvilles who held it and the manorial rights until 1371 when it passed to Sir John Aylesbury from whose family it went to George Evelyn in 1595.

Between the manor house and the churchyard is the manorial pound into which the owner of the manor and any member of the Evelyn family has right of entry—not that there are nowadays any cattle there to inspect. Close to it there was once a barn, but this was demolished in the 1920s and painstakingly reconstructed at the Burford Bridge Hotel—an interesting English example of the custom quite prevalent in the inter-war period whereby American millionaires dismantled castles or ancient houses stone by stone and brick by brick for re-erection in the United States; older readers may recall a René Clair film on this theme called *The Ghost Goes West*.

The new church spire peers out over the top of the slope. This is the only disagreeable part of that happy reconstruction. The tower and spire, like those at Burstow, are in regimented grey

Witley:
(above) Enton Mill, *(below)* the medieval rectory and church

(left) Misericords in
Lingfield Church
(below) The tomb of
Reginald, Lord Cobham,
in Lingfield Church

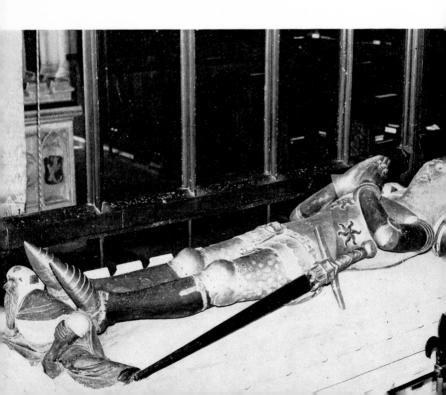

(above) Smallfield Place

(below) Lingfield Church and Close

Thursley

cedar shingles, and give the effect of a space-ship or submarine, curious in a church.

It is hardly true today to say, as a writer of 1824 could, that: "The cottage on the road-side, and the neighbouring common, furnish many interesting scenes of humble life; and the native simplicity and inoffensive manners of their inhabitants well bespeak the true characteristics of the English peasant—

> 'Poor, yet industrious, modest, quiet, neat'."

That sort of peasantry, the society of the hymn—

> The rich man in his castle
> And the poor man at his gate

has disappeared and gone for ever, and probably justly, though heaven knows whether what has come to replace it is necessarily better or more just!

The church of St. James, at least, is certainly a finer place now than it was then, better too than it was after a major reconstruction in 1857. A comparison of the present building with old prints and drawings makes this clear. This happy situation is owed to disaster, to two disasters indeed, that cleared away the lumber of centuries and the taste of 1857.

In August 1944 a flying bomb, landing in a nearby orchard, almost completely destroyed the Early English church built almost certainly on a pre-Conquest site. The careful reconstruction was lovingly and imaginatively directed by F. Etchells, but, nearly twenty years later, in the summer of 1964, lightning struck the tower and fire added to this second disaster. The repairs were again expertly handled and the result is superb, one of the most lovely of village churches. It is fortunate that this is an active parish and there has been no lack of funds and generous donors to support the work.

The main impression is of light, the light of off-white walls without the dazzling, hygienic brilliance of, say, Burstow, of three shapely lancets at the east end of the chapel filled with clear glass and noble trees outside and daylight, and of the fine Renaissance-style window, again of clear glass, at the west end of the nave. The nave furnishings are of light oak, and the chapel is almost bare of

H

seating, an attractive open space with a simple altar, three Caroline armchairs, dark against the light walls, and a great chest, some 350 years old, with panels of Gothic tracery and three shields. All these give a feeling of solidity and permanence to this spacious interior.

The east window of the chancel, again of three lancets, is filled now with the gorgeous colours of some superb modern stained glass. Here elemental shapes, a cross rising from the flames, amid the prime colours of life and the countryside, vivid blues, reds, yellows and whites, create a striking effect. This is the very best style of contemporary design, reminiscent of some of the splendid work of post-war French artists in, say, Tours. It was created by Laurence Lee. It appears, in fact, that Sir Edward Beddington Behrens offered to present a John Piper for that window but that the Church Council could not agree to accept the gift. They could not have had a happier alternative.

In the porch has been set an alabaster crucifixion, probably fifteenth-century work carved in Leicestershire which was the centre of a remarkable medieval industry in these *objets d'art* with export outlets all over Europe. This one is beautiful, Devonshire cream fashioned in uncompromising, self-confident style; the various figures, the Christ, the three Maries, the Knight and the Man of Property all have definite individuality, and the end of the two robbers crucified with Christ is tellingly and simply foretold. It is a perfect specimen. Now there are two more waiting to join it. Mrs. Clarke, of the manor, showed them to us as they awaited their setting in the church. What added wealth for this perfect little building!

Abinger sprawls through some magnificent countryside. Here and there amid the beechwoods you catch a glimpse, or a longer look, of ancient farmhouses, their interiors now doubtless equipped with every expensive device for modern living, and the country houses built in the eighteenth and nineteenth centuries by prosperous London businessmen.

To the west of the common lies the valley in which is the hamlet of Felday with some splendid houses, notably Sutton Place Farm and its attendant cottages. Out of this was carved, in 1879, the present well-known village of Holmbury St. Mary, that part of Felday with its handsome cottages and two old inns that stand around the new church. This was built, at that time, by G. E. Street in memory of his wife. It is a good building in local stone and sits rather beautifully against the surrounding hills.

Towards the north-east a lovely road skirts the upper heights of Leith Hill through woodlands decked with bluebells in spring and with rhododendrons a little later. It leads to Coldharbour, not much more than a hamlet, with a church now part of Abinger's cure. There have been a number of rather romantic theories about the origin of the name, which indeed is found widely used throughout the country. One that we recently found, unexpectedly, in an account of the American Civil War, links it with a hostelry in Roman times that provided only cold collations. It seems to us much more likely that it was simply a refuge for animals in winter weather. This one lies just behind one of the old pre-Roman earthworks, Anstiebury Camp, that guarded the southern edge of the greensand heights. Apart from this it is a picturesque place with one or two attractive cottages and a pub, the 'Plough', that has been well enlarged and furnished.

Here and there in these rolling hills are set other tiny communities. One of these, down in a valley and nestling beside a lake, is Friday Street, a small haven of real peace with an excellent restaurant, the 'Stephen Langton'. The name of Friday is presumed to indicate something unfortunate, connected with the day of the Crucifixion, a bad day or an unproductive area. This may have been true once but assuredly there can be few places pleasanter now.

A branch of the Tillingbourne runs down northwards from Friday Street through the grounds of Wotton House, once the home of the Evelyn family, whose grounds were laid out by the diarist himself. The house is only a woebegone relic of its past glory and now houses a training establishment of the fire brigade, while the church, beyond the A25, although still containing Norman elements is a dull and musty little building.

Much more rewarding, a mile or two beyond Abinger Hammer, is Shere.

Shere has some considerable claim to be regarded as the loveliest village in Surrey, especially since a by-pass has been built diverting from its narrow streets the traffic using the Dorking-Guildford road. Certainly St. James' church is one of the finest in the county.

This church has been beautifully restored between 1956 and 1966. The combination of all the finer points of the old building with the clean modernism of the present chancel and of the altar frontal and crucifix makes a really superb effect.

There is a strong idea that there was a church on this site as long ago as the seventh century and certainly a Saxon church is written about in Domesday Book (1087). The village was then called Essira. It was not until the end of the twelfth century that the present church was built in the Early English style.

Later in the century the church was connected with Netley Abbey near Southampton whose abbot was lord of the manor of Gomshall Netley. Some changes were carried out in the church during this period and more were effected a century later during the reign of Richard II. We have to wait until 1500, however, before church accounts begin and another forty-seven years before the registers commence. With the final acceptance of Protestantism in the reign of Elizabeth I, Shere church settled down into a peaceful routine uninterrupted by anything more startling than an occasional episcopal visitation or the erection of an unfortunate (architecturally) west gallery in 1748. In 1861 came a graver threat when Victorian restorers cast covetous eyes upon the building; fortunately, their depredations here were comparatively modest so that the restorers of the 1930s were able to concentrate upon checking the serious ravages of the death-watch beetle. The Second World War interrupted this vital work which was resumed in 1946 and then, when the fabric was sound again, Mr. Louis Osman, F.R.I.B.A., was entrusted with the beautification of the church in 1956. It is the splendid results of his work that the visitor sees today.

A remarkable amount of the original twelfth-century building survives, while the St. Nicholas chapel was added about 1275, at the same time as the south aisle was extended eastwards. The magnificent west doorway is even earlier than the St. Nicholas chapel and the door itself is dated 1626. Far older is the massive door in the south doorway: it is of oak and probably was made around 1200. The doorways themselves offer interesting stylistic contrasts: the arch of the south has excellent decoration in the Norman style, while the west is in the Early English style. There are scratched pilgrims' crosses on the south doorway.

In the chancel are monumental brasses, one dedicated to Robert Scarcliff, rector of the parish, who died in 1412. Three hundred years after his death, the rector was Thomas Duncombe whose incumbency began in 1658 and lasted for fifty-six years. Since there were five Duncombes after him, the last of whom died in 1805, students of eighteenth-century history will hardly be surprised to learn that the gift of the living was in the hands of the Duncombe family!

In 1955, as photographs show only too clearly, the chancel was a sadly cluttered affair, lacking space and light. Mr. Osman's efforts have utterly transformed it; the ornate altar rails and the clumsy choir stalls have disappeared, as has the old altar and the curtains on each side of it; church banners have been discreetly placed elsewhere in the building, carpets removed from the floor and the walls painted a pure white. The effect is both remarkable and aesthetically delightful, a superb example of tactful modernization.

The Purbeck marble font of the thirteenth century was restored in 1955 with the same loving skill as went into the general rehabilitation begun the following year; the crusader alms coffer dates from the same period as the font, whilst the bells (now six in number) and the chalice are Tudor in origin, the chalice being dated 1569.

We have left to the end one of the most remarkable features of this glorious church—the anchoress's cell in the north wall. In 1329 Christine Carpenter, whose father was the carpenter of Shere, expressed a desire to be an anchoress, perpetually walled up in a tiny cell, cut off from the sun and from the company of all living things, able only to follow the service of Mass through a tiny aperture. The Bishop of Winchester gave Christine the desired permission, but it is clear that rigorous confinement proved too harsh for her since we find that the Bishop in 1332 issued another document containing these words: "now forswearing this life and conduct that she assumed, she has left her cell inconstantly and returned to the world". The Bishop was prepared to allow her to re-enter her cell but on condition that she was guarded "with suitable solicitude and competent vigilance" to ensure that "the said Christine shall not wander from the laudable intention otherwise solemnly undertaken and again run about being torn to pieces by the attacks of the Tempter". We must assume, therefore, that the carpenter's daughter ended her life in the insanitary confinement of that tiny cell.

Opposite the lich-gate of the church, across the pleasant house-lined square, is The White Horse Inn which dates from the sixteenth century but has been refronted. In the village are numerous houses of antiquity, all making a cumulative effect of beauty.

Albury is quaint and it has a curious history. The old village, and the name means just that, stood contentedly and fruitfully on a large expanse of Folkestone Beds where Albury Park now is. The owners, named Godschall, were powerful enough towards the end of the eighteenth century to enclose the whole area and so to dispossess the inhabitants, who gradually moved outside the park to establish the present community. Only the ancient church remained.

Not long after the Napoleonic Wars the property was bought by Henry Drummond who was an 'apostle' of the Catholic Apostolic Church, one of those strange sects that are always apt to flourish. He caused the old church to fall into disuse, and, instead, provided two churches: that of the parish in the village, a large red-brick building with a rather handsome interior, and the impressive stone Apostolic church that stands on a knoll on the eastern approaches to the village. Both these were built in 1842 and, unbelievably, are both by the same architect, Brooks. The Apostolic church is a mysterious place; it is in good condition, carefully swept and garnished and containing some good examples of nineteenth-century glass and some lovingly carved pew-ends, and, indeed, it is a fine building; but it has not been used for a service during the last twenty years. It is kept locked but the custodian in the cottage next door is quite willing to open it.

The ancient church is a pitiable work, dilapidated and mouldering. There is some original Saxon work in it, notably at the base of the tower where the lower two-light window is certainly of that period. Round the north door, too, is some Saxon herring-bone work. The porch is Tudor and one of the roses is still visible, and most of the interior was built about 1280, though the south chapel, which became the mortuary chapel of the Drummond family, was rebuilt by Pugin in the 1840s. The decoration is still fairly well-preserved. Only a wall or two remain of the chancel in which a small sycamore flaunts its youth. It is a melancholy place, the more so now that it is totally neglected and approached only by a muddy track.

The park was laid out by John Evelyn, at the request of the Earl of Arundel, and some of the great trees he planted are still standing, though the house is now in the hands of a development company who are turning it into several flats.

The present village is not unattractive and it gains interest through the series of tall, twisted chimneys that seem to be Pugin's main characteristic as an architect here. After all he was better known as the decorator of Barry's Houses of Parliament. It is a booming place now with industry, laboratories and development companies moving in.

Near this pleasant village in the Tillingbourne Valley William Cobbett was born. Aubrey called the area "a little romancy vale" and Cobbett himself remarked of it that it was a place "where no rigour of seasons can ever be felt". In 1822, however, on one of his rural rides, he expressed himself vigorously on the subject of Chilworth where were manufactured two "of the most damnable inventions that ever sprang from the minds of man under the influence of the devil! namely, the making of gunpowder and banknotes!"

The gunpowder works were, even in 1822, of considerable antiquity, having been founded by the Evelyn family in the 1570s; a century later, there were sixteen mills which had dwindled to one by 1912. In 1970 no modern Cobbett will be offended by the presence of either devilish inventions in Chilworth: banknotes have long since ceased to begin their mundane career in these rustic surroundings.

Bereft of its two major industries, Chilworth today has been swamped by some 'overspill' from Godalming and Guildford. It can boast of at least one fine house, Chilworth Place, the origins of which appear to go back to Saxon times when the manor was held by a certain Alwin. From him it passed in 1066 to that redoubtable cleric Bishop Odo of Bayeux, no doubt as part of his reward for his services to the Norman cause at Hastings in which battle he apparently wielded with deadly effect that extraordinary weapon known as a holy-water sprinkler; this was much favoured by militant clerics as its main purpose was to break skulls, a procedure which avoided the spilling of blood deplored by canon law.

There is a theory that Chilworth house was later a cell of Newark Priory but this has been dismissed by Mr. Wilfred Hooper. Certitude comes with the knowledge that Sir Edward Randyll built a new house on the original site in the early seventeenth century; he used stone with rubbed brick dressings on the south front, adding to it a handsome central porch with a shaped brick gable. In 1664 his descendant, Vincent, the gunpowder maker, was assessed for tax on thirteen hearths, indicating a house of considerable size. It was this Randyll who created the terraced garden which today is such a delight.

In 1720 the house was bought for £30,000 by Richard Houlditch who must soon have regretted his costly purchase, for he lost all his money when the South Sea Bubble burst and was compelled to sell Chilworth Place to no less a person than Sarah, widow of the great Duke of Marlborough. She had the fine north front added and may have designed the curious pilasters on its upper part. This front is in the classical style and is of red brick; the windows seen today are a Regency addition. Cobbett recorded that the house was in considerable decay in his time and it was not rescued from this decay until it was restored by Mr. Mildmay in the 1930s. In 1945 it became the home of Sir Lionel Heald, whose kindness has enabled the present authors to enjoy a visit to it.

The eighteenth-century drawing-room on the ground floor has all the spaciousness and dignity that one expects in domestic design of this period, and it is reached by 'the green passage', a delightful long gallery with cream paint and a green carpet. A similar gallery is found above it on the first floor on which there are fourteen bedrooms, some of which contain fine early nineteenth-century iron grates. The domestic offices on the ground floor are of a size to be expected in a house of this type, in which there was once a veritable hierarchy of servants from the butler downwards, not to mention ten gardeners. Nowadays one gardener tends the fine lawns and the numerous flower-beds while the indoor staff has been proportionately reduced.

Southwards of this part of the Tillingbourne Valley the greensand hills rise to a somewhat waterless waste of heathland with few settlements of any size today. At one time, however, there was a very considerable Roman centre on Farley Heath. This must have been the largest Roman establishment in Surrey for it contained a sizeable temple and a branch of Stane Street ran up from Rowhook to it.

Nothing now remains of the Roman buildings. Too many inexpert hands have dug for spoil and what might have been another Fishbourne has been destroyed for ever.

In King John's day the road clearly extended further westwards than Farley Heath down to the ford at Shalford (shallow ford), which is far too close to Guildford to have preserved much of its village atmosphere. There are, however, some attractive houses and a fine eighteenth-century water-mill.

Wonersh once rejoiced in the name of Wogheners; it seems that its first church was built in the eleventh century when the village was simply a hamlet and part of Shalford. It became a parish in its own right in the thirteenth century and it was then that the chancel of the church was rebuilt and the tower added. This tower can still be seen today and it is remarkably unspoilt by its later additions.

Between 1250 and 1450 many changes were made in Wonersh church and the unusual crypt or sacristy dates from this period. This is reached via a doorway in the chancel and a few modern steps—for the crypt is about 5 feet below the level of the church. Aubrey wrote that it was "strongly barricaded with iron . . . to preserve the copes, plate and sacred utensils from sacrilege" but more modern writers consider that it may have been a store-room, a charnel-house (surely not placed so near the chancel?) or a room for keeping relics (surely any such would have been proudly displayed rather than locked away in a pseudo-crypt?).

In the fifteenth century the north chapel was built; this cut the crypt in half, the eastern portion, however, surviving as a lean-to outside the chapel; this vanished when the church was comprehensively—and very intelligently—restored in 1901.

The north chapel opens to the chancel with a beautiful fifteenth-century arch, more elaborate than its contemporary made to cut through the east wall of the tower. Not the least interesting feature of this north chapel is the squint, the sill of which is, unusually, a piscina. The font at the opposite end of the chapel is largely made of a Norman bowl and stem, disinterred in 1901 and repaired. There is a font-cover. Near the font is a sixteenth-century tomb of Sussex marble though it is not known whose sepulchre it is.

The chancel has much of architectural interest and beauty. The screen on the south side is made up of two fifteenth-century screens; that on the north side dates from the 1901 restoration. The splendid tie-beam in the chancel is grooved on its underside, suggesting the existence once of a further partition in addition to the rood screen which was formerly in place beneath the chancel arch with a solid tympanum above it.

The chancel floor has two good brasses, one of them commemorating a certain Henry Biyot who died in 1503, his wife and their twenty-three children, twelve boys and eleven girls; the sanctuary floor has two brass-plates with Gothic inscriptions inserted into it and all this is lit by a superb Flemish chandelier; for Communion services, the church has a fine Elizabethan chalice, the cover of which is a paten.

The organ is on the south side of the chancel and behind it is a good seventeenth-century tomb with fine carving; here is buried a Filezar (a legal officer who filed writs in the Court of Common Pleas) of the city of London. Honesty compels the admission that this tomb was, on the occasion of our visit, serving the purpose of a table upon which various vases, kettles and other homely utensils were haphazardly placed. In a church as well kept as this, it should surely be possible to find an alternative resting-place for these impedimenta so that the interested visitor may inspect this tomb (which features in the church's guide book) without the distraction they provide.

Wonersh church has the most beautiful surroundings, a graveyard impeccably kept and surrounded by an aged wall, a doorway through which leads to the green. This attractive area was presented to the village by a local lady in 1935 and subsequently placed in perpetual trust for its use. Quiet (despite the proximity of the main road), this green, suitably provided with rustic seats, should be a welcome place of repose for the aged people of Wonersh.

The restoration of the church was, as had been said, carried out with care and skill in 1901; one shudders to think what the Victorians might have done to it, perhaps thirty years earlier. Particularly skilful was the way in which the features of outstanding interest in the old building (mostly those which had luckily survived a three-year period of total neglect in the early eighteenth century) were incorporated into the restored edifice. Inside, the result is wholly admirable, but the exterior is undeniably marred by a hideous red-brick porch and by some clumsy restoration, also in red brick, of the outer fabric close to the tower.

Wonersh was once a centre of the weaving industry and weavers' beams can still be seen in some of the old cottages which are such a delightful feature of the village today. Aubrey wrote that the villagers themselves caused the decline of their trade by unduly stretching the cloth, to the understandable displeasure of their customers. Like many Surrey villages, Wonersh now has no particular trade.

In 1970 Wonersh was awarded first prize in the competition for the best-kept large village in Surrey, an honour well deserved if our observation of it on three visits is anything to go by. The 'Grantley Arms', basically a half-timbered building, stands nobly at the centre of the village and dispenses excellent refreshment, as it always has. It is named after the Grantley family who owned so much of the neighbourhood, including Great Tangley Manor, in the nineteenth century. The Manor, hidden away up its private road, is considered one of the finest Elizabethan houses still standing in the county.

Another of the Grantley holdings was Bramley.

Before the Conquest and for some time after it, Bramley gave its name to one of the most powerful and largest manors in Surrey. This stretched from Shalford to the Sussex border and included great tracts of the Weald forest, untenanted then but later to become villages, manors in their own right, like Dunsfold and Alfold. This vast manor had been laid, under Harold, by one Alnod Cild, and William awarded it to the battling Bishop Odo of Bayeux. It was not long before it became forfeit to the Crown, and from Henry I's time onward Bramley fell on evil days; the manor was divided into smaller parts used to reward successful time-servers and fighting men. It remained divided until the beginning of the nineteenth century when William, Lord Grantley managed, by purchase mostly, to reunite the greater part of it.

The name, Bramley, gives little clue to its origin, it may stand for broom-covered clearing, or, conceivably, for brown pasture. The present village straggles beside one of the main tributaries of the Wey, on good sandy soil, and was certainly established because of its fertility. There are a number of fine houses and cottages in the village itself and in the hamlet of Thorncombe. Bramley East Manor, in the High Street, is a fine sixteenth-century building and it stands opposite another half-timbered house. Other houses opposite the church are spoiled by a multiplicity of traffic signs.

The church is unattractive. The presence of a church here is noted in Domesday, and then it was one of three in the confines of the manor. Later, however, it was purely a chapel under Shamley. In 1844, by Act of Parliament, it became a separate parish and almost at once the business of restoration was launched. The insides were torn apart, windows inserted with contemporary glass, a north aisle was built, to be followed by a south aisle in 1875. In all this, whatever remained from the past was destroyed and a memorial was erected to Victorian taste in the fabric and to Victorian social philosophy in a tablet set in the north aisle that reads: "A.D. 1850. This aisle was built without cost to the parishioners to the glory of God and for the benefit of the poor inhabitants of Bramley for whose use the seats are to remain free forever".

Now the village is a prosperous dormitory community. There is an upstage girls' school, a decaying railway line and station, a busy flow of traffic and strings of small children, mostly female, in jodhpurs and black velvet caps astride fat ponies, a charming sight!

South of Bramley the greensand rises again to the heights of Hascombe Hill that suddenly drops very steeply to the Wealden clay. Its position and its steepness made this a natural site for a Neolithic hill fort. Three sides are naturally fortified and ditches protect the fourth. Some flint arrow-heads and stone querns have been dug up there. A path leads to it from behind the pub in the centre of the village, which is sited picturesquely in the valley which gave it its name, possibly 'brushwood valley'.

Apart from a little modern development Hascombe preserves a pleasantly rural air with the timelessness of old cottages. Outwardly the church fits in, although it is a complete rebuilding of 1864 by H. Woodyer in a sort of Early English style. Inside, however, it is lavishly decorated in a semi-Byzantine, semi-Romanesque manner, very highly coloured like a Neopolitan ice-cream. The screen, of Jerusalem olive-wood, is of the fifteenth century and there is a square font of 1690. The rest is Woodyer. In the churchyard are several great square eighteenth-century tombs set so irregularly that they might have been the back-cloth for Stanley Spenser's "Resurrection".

All round the locality are some splendid houses. Standing a little below the level of the Godalming road, for instance, is the superb half-timbering of Winkworth Farm, three sides of a square round a picture-book courtyard and with wistaria over the façade. This gives its name to Winkworth Arboretum, an area of 99 acres owned by the National Trust, planted with flowering trees and shrubs that give a lovely display of colour in late spring, and leading down to two lakes. Not far to the north of that is the hamlet of Thorncombe Street where there is a beautiful sixteenth-century house with handsomely carved gable-ends.

A narrow lane that leads out north-eastward from Hascombe past Scotsland Farm will repay a leisurely drive; it is almost unspoilt in its rusticity and there are some fine buildings dotted along its length.

At Hambledon, a long and roundabout journey over the empty greensand hills to the west, there are some good cottages, notably Malthouse Cottage and the Malthouse Farm, of the sixteenth and seventeenth centuries. The School Cottage is even earlier. The church, however, is a rather mean structure of 1846.

It is an old manor. Before the Conquest it was held by one Azor, and William awarded it to the Salisbury family and it remained in the honour of the Earls of Salisbury. Iron was worked here and bricks were made, and it appears briefly in history when, in 1570, the villagers fought, unavailingly it seems, against Lord Montague who was cutting commonland trees down to provide fuel for his iron-works. Otherwise it has led a comparatively peaceful existence, and peace is its key-note today.

7

Greensand 3 (West)

L I K E a knife-edge the thin chalk line of the Hog's Back sticks out from Guildown to the confines of Farnham. This is the ancient trackway of pre-Roman times, called at various times the Via Regia and the Harow Way. Beyond Guildford it becomes the so-called 'Pilgrims' Way', but it is far older than an association with the St. Thomas cult at Canterbury. The sides of the Hog's Back are steep and under it and sheltered by it is another narrow strip of the fertile greensand. Along this is a line of primitive settlements lying under another, now more rustic way.

The parishes lying below the Hog's Back stretched out, as did those all along the edge of the chalk downs, up on to the hills and down into the forest, thus obtaining grazing rights for sheep on the downs and provender for pigs among the trees, which also yielded fuel for the fires. Compton is one of these, the nearest to Guildford, its name signifying the 'valley farmstead'.

The parish church shows something of its age, but there is no doubt that a settlement existed here from earliest times. Relics of Neolithic man have been found in various parts, and remains of a Roman villa, of which nothing now can be seen, were discovered in the northern end of the parish.

Parts of the church are of Saxon construction and most of the rest of it is Norman, and good Norman at that, with some magnificent arch-mouldings and pillar-capitals. This is not all; unique in Britain, Compton has a two-storey chancel, a vaulted sanctuary below and a chapel above it, built into the previous chancel in about 1180, the walls simply being thickened a little to absorb the additional thrust. Along the upper chapel runs a simple wooden railing with round-headed openings which are cut from one single, massive plank and are mounted on octagonal shafts. A simple railing, except that it is as old as the structure on which it stands, a piece of Norman carpentry. Under it runs a flattened round arch decorated with deeply cut horseshoe moulding with dog-tooth round the edge. From this the vaulting of the sanctuary runs back to support the chapel.

Little enough seems to be known about the early history of the building and it is intriguing to speculate on the reasons for the making of this two-storey chancel. It appears likely that, for some reason, Compton was an especially holy place. There is a tiny square window low down behind the rector's stall, seen better from outside, on the north side, which probably belonged to a hermit's cell that may have stood there before the Conquest. On the south side, facing that, is a small two-storey chamber, in which is now the staircase to the upper chapel, and which, again, was almost certainly a hermit's cell. From it opens a cross-shaped squint that would give a kneeling holy man a sight of the Mass. Beyond this the oak board of the sill shows the depressions made by constant use. The nameless tomb on the north side of the chancel was found to contain several skeletons, one with flaming red hair, and it has been suggested that these were successive occupants of the anchorite's cell. This all makes it tempting to suppose that there must have been some special significance about this church, some holy relics perhaps, that required a special display place, and that it was for this that the double structure was made.

The tower is probably pre-Conquest, as are parts of the nave walls and of the chancel. In the lower chancel the piscina and the aumbry are early Norman, and so is the piscina that was moved into the upper chapel when it was constructed. The aisles and the arcade joining them to the nave are Norman, the arches, like the main chancel arch, built of clunch. Here the pillar capitals are of strongly carved foliage designs, and the underside of the arches, and, here and there, the face of the arches, as elsewhere, have designs incised into the thin plaster, a highly decorative effect produced by these repeating motifs. The window of the lower

Puttenden Manor

Outwood Mill

Village cricket at Outwood

Cottages on Stane Street, Ockley

sanctuary is early Norman, and the lancets at the west end of the chancel are early English of the first period, about 1180.

Round the arch of the chancel is painted in red ochre a design of cubes, and the roof of the chancel dates from 1165. From the south aisle is a squint partially hidden by the Caroline pulpit with its inlaid diamond patterning and a canopy. The communion table and the altar rail are also of the seventeenth century. At the west end now is an oak screen of the same period that used to stand across the chancel arch.

What is modern here? Well, in the fifteenth century the roof of the south aisle was raised, and the windows were inserted into the wall. The porch came in the last century, as did the pews and the dormer windows. In 1953 some restoration was carried out carefully and the basic building was preserved, a wonderful and rewarding church to savour at leisure.

There are one or two sound examples of sixteenth-century building in the parish, notably the White House, formerly the White Hart Inn, near the church, and the cottages at Polstead Manor.

A little to the north of the village, standing on a hillock linked by legend with an apocryphal defeat of the French in the twelfth century, you will see a tall cruciform building in red brick. This may remind you vaguely of a village church in the northern Lombardy plain, or of a small Greek Orthodox chapel. It is, in fact, a memorial chapel to the artist, G. F. Watts, and was erected in 1896 to designs by the artist's widow. It is an astonishing creation which cannot fail to produce violent feelings. The narrow arms of the cross-shaped building rise sheer, high, to widely overhanging eaves, and round the semicircular arch of the doorway are cut creatures that recall the beasts that adorn the Norman church of Kilpeck in Herefordshire.

Inside, round the small, circular area, great angels in dull greens and reds stand guard, for all the world like Aztec gods, and cherubs' heads peer out from between them, amid a leaf design. Here one can see something of the influence of Raphael. Everywhere are stucco whorls and heads all mingled with the opening words of St. John's Gospel. In its way it is striking, but it is striking in much the same manner as a 'space spectacular' in cinerama.

I

Outside is a small cemetery, used now by the villagers. Just beside that is a field full of Highland cattle, seeming to be looking wistfully for Landseer to paint them.

Not far away from there, down the valley, is a well-designed and well-organized gallery of Watts' work. It is interesting to look at this display of a large number of his paintings for they cover such a wide range of styles and of attitudes. This simpering purity of the Burne-Jones maidens is there, but so is powerful portraiture with echoes of Rembrandt or of Hals in its authority and power.

Just before moving west along the line of the Hog's Back, we want to look in on Wanborough, which, in true fact, does not fit into this chapter at all. Indeed, it does not fit into any of the chapters since it, alone of all the villages, sits on the chalk on the north of this narrow ridge. However, it has such close associations with the south side and even, at one place, extends over the ridge into the greensand, that it has a place here.

It is tiny, a handful of houses, and its church is tiny, a single cell measuring only 45 feet by 18, and even that was, from 1674 to 1861, used as a granary or stable. When it was brought back into service there was some restoration, of course, and the west wall had to be rebuilt, but it has hardly been touched. The fabric is mostly of the thirteenth century, although the square-framed east window was inserted in the fifteenth. There are lancets of the original building, and a piscina and a large opening that may have been a credence recess or an aumbry, and it has an early arch-braced roof with a moulded centre rib, which is unusual.

The manor existed at the time of Domesday and was awarded at the Conquest to Geoffrey de Mandeville, one of whose successors wrote one of the earliest of travel books, his, unlike, of course, its modern progeny, being mostly fictitious! In 1130 Wanborough was sold to Waverley Abbey and the monks, by the time the church was built, had obtained the privilege of holding an annual fair here on the feast of St. Bartholomew, to whom the church is dedicated. They too, without doubt, constructed the great tithe barn that quite dwarfs the tiny church. This barn was built between 1350 and 1400 and is enormous. When it was repaired recently it was reckoned that there were 32,000 tiles on the roof. The timbers, however, look as though they had been used before, possibly in ships, as they have grooves and clefts in them that are no part of their present use.

The manor house, beside the church, bears the date 1527, but it is quite clearly a later building, Jacobean in style. Exactly why it has that date on the front is as yet a mystery. Mystery goes with it; during the last war it was used as a training place for agents who were to be dropped into Occupied Europe. Perhaps M.I.5 put the false date on the house to deceive the enemy!

South again is Puttenham. This possesses a good church, dedicated to St. John the Baptist, and many beautiful old houses and cottages. It is also fortunate in having a very active local history society, members of which have compiled a most informative guide to the church and have also carried out much interesting research into the history of the village.

Unhappily, the church was badly restored in 1868 (John Betjeman's famous parody of "The Church's One Foundation" is aptly reproduced in the guide) but a Norman north arcade and a Norman window in the south wall still remain, the tower is very early fifteenth century and the chancel has a brass of Edward Cranford who was rector from 1400 until 1431. A much more recent memorial records the tragic death of a young man called Hugh Pope who was killed while climbing in the Pyrenees. He was alone at the time and a party had to go from England to find his body; this party included Claude Elliott, later Provost of Eton, and Arnold Lunn, a pioneer in winter sports and mountaineering. Only 23 at the time of his death in 1912, Hugh Pope was buried at Orthez.

In the north aisle is a memorial to Esther Bellasis whose parents John King and Mary (*née* Budd) are buried in the churchyard. The Budds were an interesting local family whose female members were distinguished for their beauty and for the freedom with which they bestowed their favours upon young men of the district. Esther, however, married Captain George Bellasis of the East India Company's army and was joined in Bombay by two of her sisters in 1800. One of these sisters was jilted by a young man who was then killed in a duel by Bellasis. Since duelling was by this time a crime, Bellasis was sentenced to fourteen years' transportation to Botany Bay and Esther returned home to die of a broken heart in 1805. Her husband was released after only five years of his sentence and on his return to England erected the memorial to his wife. He then married his wife's sister Eliza, herself a widow, and lived happily with her in India until his death in the 1820s.

Five female Budds in the years between 1813 and 1839 are recorded as the mothers of bastards; in no cases are the fathers mentioned.

Papers read at meetings of the Puttenham and Wanborough History Society are the source of the story of the Budd girls and also contain much excellent information about the old houses in the village, such as Winter's Farm (*c.* 1400), Rosemary Cottage (*c.* 1480) and the Old Cottage (*c.* 1490); of the sixteenth century are Farm Cottage and Street Farm, whose fine chimney was added at the beginning of the seventeenth century. On the outskirts of the village as it is approached from Seale are Rodsall and Shoelands, both of which are very handsome brick houses of the Jacobean period. Mrs. Dugmore, the authority on the old houses of Puttenham, has some very interesting comments upon the change over from wood to brick which is a feature of the domestic architecture of the early seventeenth century. She ascribes the change to a developing shortage of wood (a shortage which incidentally was very worrying to those concerned with the Royal Navy), and to the developing influence of the Dutch whose traders were very frequent visitors to England at this time and whose houses in the United Provinces were increasingly in brick. Prosperous yeoman farmers imitated their social superiors and there are a number of brick houses built by them in Puttenham still, the School House and No. 58, The Street, being examples. Mrs. Dugmore rightly admires the handsome Georgian Step Cottage (with three storeys, cottage is perhaps not quite the *mot juste* for this fine dwelling) and the Regency Manor House of 1824.

Puttenham has had its fair share of alarums and excursions during its long history since the Saxon days when it was 'Putta's home'. Even earlier, it had been colonized by mesolithic man who found that it was situated on the fertile greensand and who also appreciated its sheltered position. The name is first mentioned as Potenham in 1191, the present spelling not appearing until the fourteenth century. Throughout, Puttenham has remained very small because it is neither on a river nor on a trade route; for a very long time, most of the county south of it was thick forest. Its small population was severely afflicted by plague in 1603 (this must have been the outbreak which caused James I to postpone his coronation and his first parliament until 1604 because of its virulence in London) and in the Civil War Parliamentary troops from Farnham Castle occupied the village, whose people welcomed the return of Charles II and of their former rector Henry Beedell in 1660 with great rejoicing. In April 1735 in the village black-smith's shop a serious fire broke out which destroyed some cottages and badly damaged the church. The devoted energies of one of the churchwardens, Ralph Toft, effected the necessary restoration of the church very quickly, aided by generous gifts in money and materials from neighbouring, and London, churches.

Not even this fire, however, was so destructive as were the well-meaning Victorian restorers of the late 1860s: down went the east end, out went most of the windows, in went a new pulpit, a new font and, *horrible dictu*, the tiles in the nave. The stark simplicity revealed in a series of water colours by John Hassell between 1820 and 1830 gave way to the usual clutter with which the Victorians delighted to fill old churches. Fortunately, the very recent work has done much to bring light and spaciousness to the building, enabling the visitor to see something of the surviving ancient features.

Halfway along the country road that runs towards Seale is the fine seventeenth-century complex of East End Farm. Although modern riches have been used to refabricate much of the old struc-ture, this is a splendid example of the prosperous building of the later Stuart period.

Seale itself is a little disappointing. It has a wonderful position set on rolling, hilly country, picturesquely ideal. Almost nothing could spoil it, and yet it is dull. The church, originally thirteenth century and possibly a pilgrims' chapel of ease, was 'prettified' in 1860–61, when the tower was heightened and given a low spire, when the nave was enlarged and a new east window was put in, when the vestry was added, and when the fabric was given a 'face-lift'. Some elements of the old church can still be found, the early thirteenth-century font and some lancets of about the same period, the fifteenth-century porch, a few six-teenth- and seventeenth-century brasses, some hatchments and the fragment of a fourteenth-century breviary preserved in the vestry. Over the altar is a painting attributed to Giovanni Battista Cima (1489–1517), an artist of the Venetian School, representing John the Baptist, the Virgin and Child, and St. Catherine.

Just beside the church is the Manor Farm, a sound, solid and unexciting building of the eighteenth century.

As to the origin of the name, Seale, the experts are not at one. One version refers to it as the word 'sele', meaning a hall or building, and another suggests a connection with willows (Saxon 'sealh' that persists in the word 'sallow', or 'sally' willow). Our suggestion would connect it with the Old English 'sael', time or happy occasion, that itself has connections with 'selig' meaning holy. South of here, and linked by an ancient way from this station on the ancient trackway of the Hog's Back, is an area conceivably dedicated to various Saxon gods, a holy place: Thursley, Tuesley, Peper Harow certainly suggest this, and maybe Elstead as well.

From the time of the Norman kings onward, most of Seale came within the manor of Tongham, which lies on the other side of the Hog's Back. The root of the name of Tongham is, it seems, precisely what it says, i.e. 'tongs'. The philologist suggests that this may refer to a fork in the river, but much more likely, we feel, is that it describes this region that straddles the sharp ridge of the Hog's Back.

Of the two monasteries which remain in a ruined state in Surrey, Waverley is certainly the more interesting. This Cistercian house was founded as early as 1128 and was the first Cistercian monastery in England. It flourished so greatly that, a century after its foundation, it housed 70 monks and over 100 lay brothers and had been very considerably extended. A huge church was begun in 1203 and not finished until 1278. Henry III favoured the order, and his support enabled the abbot to act in a very high-handed way when the abbey's shoemaker was arrested for murder and sought sanctuary at the abbey. The officers of the law who had arrested him were compelled to undergo a flogging and to ask humble pardon of the abbot, this pardon being graciously given.

There were no further legal interferences with the monastic inmates!

In 1233 a serious flooding of the River Wey did much damage and it is a curious fact that when the abbey was dissolved just over 300 years later by Henry VIII its revenue was very small, a mere £174 per annum.

The indefatigable Aubrey visited Waverley in 1673 and found the ruins quite extensive, the old chapel being then used as a stable. Today the abbey ruins are privately owned. In the summer of 1970, however, the Ministry of Works was permitted to carry out repairs to the walls of the monastery which are still standing. These include portions of the cellararium, over which was once the lay brothers' dormitory, of the church, and of one building whose exact purpose is not certain.

The River Wey winds its course most attractively through the fields adjacent to the abbey and on the opposite side to the abbey is Waverley House, rebuilt in 1833 after a fire had destroyed much of the original building. Near this is Moor Park, the home of the Temple family from 1633 and the house in which Jonathan Swift, secretary to the diplomat Sir William Temple at the end of the seventeenth century, wrote *The Tale of a Tub*. The house was considerably altered by Sir William in 1684 and was restored in the eighteenth century. Walter Scott stayed there while doing research for a life of Swift and was sufficiently attracted by the ruins of Waverley Abbey to adopt its name for the first of his historical novels. Sir Arthur Conan Doyle gave a vivid picture of life in a Cistercian abbey in his historical novel *Sir Nigel*.

Today Moor Park, where the great Swift spent such important years (there is a cottage named after his beloved Stella near the house, though it is extremely unlikely that she ever lived there), is used for adult education.

South and east from here the countryside becomes progressively more sandy and unproductive, though there are still some lovely little communities scattered along the river and the tributary streams, where the country roads wind contentedly among trees. One of these is Tilford.

There can be no doubt about the antiquity of the settlement at Tilford, though for centuries it was but a distant hamlet in the parish of Farnham. It occupies an important geographical position where two branches of the River Wey unite, and its two bridges, however ancient they may be, must inevitably mark important crossing-places from the earliest days of human habitation. Perhaps the famous oak on the north side of the green can give some sort of scale of age, for it is reckoned to be some 900 years old. It is 10 feet in diameter at its widest point, but it is much patched up and nursed in these days. Cobbett referred to it, and in 1852 the Bishop of Winchester was given lands in the village as a grant as Trustee for the preservation of the tree.

Bricks and tiles have been manufactured in the locality for a very long time; remains of a Roman kiln have been found, and some of the old cottages and farm buildings have locally made tiles.

Tilford House is a magnificent example of the best Wren style, a beautifully proportioned small country mansion, the windows exactly measured and the doorway covered by a small pediment and a flowing sundial. The stables, at the side, are arranged equally in proportion. It was erected in about 1690. Shortly after 1760 it was bought by Elizabeth Abney, who was a Presbyterian and obtained a licence to hold services there. In 1776 a chapel was built in the stable yard, but this fell into disuse by the middle of the next century. The farm on the other side of the road has fifteenth- as well as seventeenth-century work in it. Bridge Cottage, nearer the village, seems to have been enlarged upwards towards the end of the eighteenth century, and the bottom storey must be much older.

The ancient bridge there has been more than a little spoiled by the addition of a modern utilitarian companion to cater for current traffic needs. The green is a large triangle of turf, famous for its cricket pitch and not overcrowded with buildings around it. The 'Barley Mow' was built there about 1700.

The church is not old; it was raised in 1867 and is a fair example of the better architecture of the time, spacious, unencumbered by ornamentation, and it sits quietly on its hillock among trees, self-effacing.

The road to Frensham doesn't follow the river bed; it goes up through the trees and scrubland of the sandy heaths before it

drops down again into the valley where the actual village of Frensham lies, its old church commanding a parish that covers an
enormous area around.

Frensham is today best known for its scenery; large numbers
of people come to picnic (and leave their litter) beside the two
Frensham Ponds, of which the Great has an area of about 100
acres and the Little of about half that; most of the beauty spots
of Hindhead, the Devil's Jumps and the Punch Bowl, are also
officially in the parish. There are great areas of heathland, agri-
culturally unproductive but ablaze with gorse and broom in late
spring, and the hills yield tremendous views out to the Hog's Back
and into Hampshire and Sussex. It is a fine region for the walker
and has become a favourite place for comfortable middle-class
retirement, as well as for nursing homes.

The old village is quite a small place, though there are scattered
hamlets included in the parish, and it seems that it was never of
much importance. Indeed its early history is mainly conjecture,
although a church must have stood somewhere here from the very
earliest times. The first record of the church is found in the annals
of Waverley Abbey in the year 1239, but this is a record of its
being moved from its original site to its present position. The record
reads thus: "Ecclesia de Fermesham transponitur hoc anno de
loco ubi prius sita fuit ad alium locum consilio et auxilio Lucae
archidiaconi Surreiae et hoc eodem anno dedicata est." How pleasant it is to find Latin so easy to read!

The likelihood is that the old building stood up on the hill on
the other side of the River Wey. Ancient tradition has it that the
earliest Christian church in the region was built on those heights.
It may even be that this building marked the site of the battle of
893 in which Alfred's son, Edward, defeated the Danish invaders
at Farnham. This is conjecture. The date of the removal of the
church is not, and this may have had some connection with the
devastating floods of 1233 that destroyed so many local bridges
and led to compulsory orders for their rebuilding. To have the
church on the far side of the river may well have appeared foolish
in view of that disaster and have led to the decision to bring it
nearer the manor house.

The main manor of the neighbourhood was that of Frensham

Beale, whose house is only a pale and patched shadow of its former glory. Another manor was that of Pierrepont, whose great house, now a school, dates only from the heyday of Victorian wealth, 1876. In that manor was the hamlet of Millbridge which contains some pleasant old houses but which is remarkable in that, in spite of its name, there is no record of there ever having been a mill there.

The village itself straggles along what is called the Street, just to the south-east of the river where the alluvial soil makes gardening worth the effort but high enough to escape all but the worst of flooding. There is a sprinkling of good seventeenth-century houses, and the general effect is not unattractive without being striking. That is left to the church. This is set back a little in its yard and lies long, lean and narrow, like a sphinx. At the west end the fat, squat, square tower with its heavy jutting buttresses is the powerful neck and head, and the nave and chancel stretch out, pressed down against the ground. The tower was built in the fifteenth century, and the rest of the present building, except for the north aisle (1827), probably shows fairly well what the removed church looked like, at least externally. Inside the customary havoc was wrought about 1868. At least some of the medieval structure was preserved. New windows were then put into the nave, but they have on the outside one unusual feature: the hood moulds are finished, surely by some craftsman with imagination and a sense of humour, with a series of heads and small figures, a pig, a skeleton, two devils and a man with his tongue stuck out, all quite in keeping with their medieval framework.

The south doorway, with a semicircular arch, much patched, beyond the porch, is of the original building, and the wooden door may well be as old. The large square font with its solid base is probably older, maybe from the former church. Its arched decoration is badly weather-worn, hardly surprisingly since it had spent possibly centuries in the churchyard before being brought inside in 1875. At that time the mean little supports were added. The pillars of the arcade as well as the corbels of the chancel, all dating from the restoration of the last century, bear the imprint of the craftsman who made the hood moulds; the capitals are deeply carved with foliage and there is, in one, a small bird. This unknown artist's work stands out. The rest of the reconstruction has nothing to commend it; the chancel floor was raised, a great deal of fine Georgian furniture was thrown out, and a poor archway was thrust between nave and chancel where no arch, it seems, had been before. Only one thirteenth-century lancet in the north side of the chancel was preserved. At the sides of this can be seen two squared shafts ending in crocketted points and standing on paired pilasters with acanthus capitals. These are all that remain of the tomb of, it is believed, John Le Bel who died about 1340. The canopy over this tomb sufficiently covered the lancet to enable it to escape destruction, though the tomb itself disappeared.

At the back of the north aisle is the famous witch's cauldron, a great fat-bellied copper container on three legs. Legend has, of course, associated it with a known witch, Mother Ludlam, who inhabited a cave near Waverley Abbey. She was, we are told, a kindly old person who lent various articles to her neighbours when requested. She even lent her cauldron on one occasion and the borrower was late returning it, whereat, in a fit of understandable pique, the good lady refused to receive it and it was left lying outside the cave, presumably being removed from there by some forward-looking rag-and-bone man. Anyway the cauldron found its way to Frensham church. Or that is the legend. The truth is probably much less romantic, as usual, but it is not wholly without charm; probably this vast pot was intended for use at Wassail time or at village feastings known as 'Church Ales', a medieval precursor of modern 'Bun Fights' and obviously a much more enjoyable occasion.

Large tracts of the country round Hindhead are owned by the National Trust and it is possible to walk for miles over the gorse-covered hills through land thus protected, and it is all beautiful walking country. Apart from this it is a region of homes of the rich and retired; Lloyd George lived, for instance, in a great mansion near Churt.

William Cobbett wrote "those that travel on turnpike roads know nothing of England" and if we substitute motorways for turnpikes we can only agree with him. Those motorists, for example, who travel along A3 are in many cases utterly unaware that a detour of about a mile (to the west) will bring them to one of Surrey's most delightful villages, Thursley. Its name means 'the field of Thunor, the Saxon war-god', but anything more peaceful than Thursley today would be difficult to imagine. It was once a centre of the Surrey glass industry and Cobbett commended its soil as providing some of the best barley in the kingdom; there is an acacia on the minute green which was planted in commemoration of Cobbett. It cannot have changed much since his day though the church has been heavily restored. There are many old houses and cottages here, notably Bear's Barn and Emley Farm on Bowlhead Green and, near the church, The Well House, which has an eighteenth-century façade as a front for a much older building, The Old Parsonage and the group of cottages called The Hatch. Indeed, few Surrey villages have so many beautiful houses in so small an area, while there are also other excellent dwellings on the outskirts of the village like Smallbrook and the Dye House.

Thursley churchyard contains the grave of a sailor who was murdered at Hindhead in 1786; the name of the victim is unknown, but his three murderers, whom he had accompanied since meeting them at Esher and whose food and accommodation he had paid for, were sentenced to death at Kingston and hanged on Gibbett Hill, the highest point on Hindhead Common.

His sad epitaph contains these lines:

> In perfect Health and in the Flower of Age
> I fell a Victim to three Ruffians' Rage.

The enlargement and restoration of the church took place between 1860 and 1884 but, as at Ockley, certain outstanding old features survived. The remarkable beams and arches which support the bell tower and which rest upon massive oak piers are still happily in position, while the chancel arch itself is thirteenth-century. In the north wall of the chancel are Saxon windows with faint traces of painting; these windows date from the early part of the eleventh century and were only rediscovered in 1927 so that the Victorian restorers missed them. Below one of them is an oven recess once used for baking the wafers used in the Mass. In the north arcade is another Saxon window and the font is a magnificent Bargate stone tub of the eleventh century.

Thursley is one of a group of villages in this neighbourhood that seem to have been dedicated to Saxon religious observances. Out beyond Milford is the hamlet of Tuesley, a place once connected with the god, Tiw. Nearer at hand is Peper Harow, and Elstead may fit into the group.

There is no really old record of the name of Elstead. Indeed the first mention appears to be when the Bishop of Winchester granted two acres in Helestede to Waverley Abbey. It seems most improbable, however, that no named community existed here where there may well have been a mill in pre-Conquest times and where the river was from ancient times almost certainly crossed. At the same time it seems strange that the Bishop should have been granting lands here, since his estates were mostly quite a bit further west, and yet the miller, in 1208, was paying his dues to the Bishop and it is believed that Oxenford Grange, to the east, was early attached to Waverley Abbey.

All this adds up to some mystery about Elstead, a mystery in no way solved by Ekwall's assertion that the name, Elstead, derives from 'ellens stede', or the place where elder-trees grow, even though he finds the elision of the 'n' unusual. We cannot resist the temptation to take issue with him here. Certainly it is not unwonted to find a place-name referring to the trees or other crops to be found there. But elders!

This corner of Surrey must have been the centre of various religious mysteries. Peper Harow, a bare couple of miles away to to the north-east, is probably derived from 'hearg', or temple, and some sort of proper name thus 'Pippa's temple' or the 'Piper's temple', either explanation at least indicative of some sort of religious basis. Then there are Thursley and Tuesley to take into consideration.

If all that is not enough evidence for the early religious importance that may have belonged to Elstead, there is the raised road that ran southwards from Seale to the great bowl of Hindhead. The Ridge, at Seale, and Ridgeway Farm beyond Thursley, may still hold the memory of that old road. And the name Seale itself has already been discussed.

If, then, the fabric of this hypothesis is sufficiently strong to carry some further weight, we wish to hang upon it a suggestion about the origin of the word Elstead. The first mention of the place refers to it as Helestede. Now the verb 'hele' (or 'heel' or 'heal') still exists in dialect and was in common use in Spenser's day. Its meaning is given as 'to hide, or conceal, or to cover, as with a roof or thatch'. Could it be, therefore, that Elstead was once the 'hidden place' or the 'secret place'? Was it, indeed, once the centre of some mystery or the seat of some oracle?

Be that as it may, Elstead lies still mainly surrounded by sandy commons and land unfertile enough to have led, in the later Middle Ages, to a specialization in sheep. Elstead was an early centre for the processing of wool, later for the manufacture of braid. The names of the two inns, 'The Woolpack' and 'The Golden Fleece', pay tribute to this part of history.

The present bridge over the Wey is not immensely old; it may only be sixteenth-century work with a much later brick parapet put on the top; it may, however, be older work patched up to bring it up to the required strength as traffic became gradually faster and heavier. In any case, the present structure must without doubt stand in the position of some earlier bridge.

A little to the west of it is the great mill. The stately eighteenth-century house was built round a much older homestead; the beams of the Tudor structure can still be seen in the living-room in which is a fine fireplace that had been bricked up until the start of this century when the inquisitiveness of the present owner, Mrs. Bentley, then a girl, led to its uncovering.

Inside was a magnificent iron fireback that bears the Royal Coat of Arms supported by the Lion and the Red Dragon of Wales and surmounted by the flattened crown of the Tudors. The ancient spit and bacon loft are still there. The wooden mill building was burned down in 1647, quite likely by Cromwellian troops billeted in Elstead, who, underpaid, and half starved, possibly attacked the mill as a supposed repository of food. One of the earliest of fire insurances was taken out some time between 1705 and 1710 to cover the owner against a repetition of that disaster. The fire mark of the Exchange House Fire Office can be seen on the house wall, while the plate of the Sun Office, which took over the Exchange business, is on the stone mill storage building. It was not until 1881 that the mill finally closed for good, after a period when it was used first as a paper mill and then for the powering of worsted looms.

There are several other fine houses in and around the village, notably Polsted Farm up Cut Mill Lane, the old Farm House, by the Bridge, a picturesque brick and timber building much overgrown with masses of wistaria hanging over it, the Old Forge which still functions in that capacity, and various long cow-byres, especially beside the British Legion hall. A great deal of tasteless modern housing has come in, however, to spoil what must not long ago have been a pleasant country village.

The church was originally a chapel attached to Farnham and seems to date from the middle of the twelfth century. In spite of a recent rehandling (if that is the fairest word) of the chancel, the primitive church can be plainly seen through the restoration work that did take place in the last century. The basic nave and chancel arrangement is clear to see, and the placing of the ancient low shingled belfry set on very solid axed oak timbers. The roof timbers of the nave are of the fifteenth century, made up of stalwart beams and massive king-posts, and the porch, untouched by the later restorations, is a little older than that. In the most easterly window on the north side of the nave are some fragments of what would seem to be sixteenth-century glass. They may even be earlier. This is a pleasant church and houses, we are told, a lively church community. Certainly on the day we visited it it was filled with flowers after the annual flower festival, and a fine sight it was.

Some way out to the east there are two further places of interest. The first is the bridge over the Wey on the Peper Harow road. This is called Somerset Bridge and it stands near Somerset Farm. Whatever may be the exact derivation of the name, this bridge appears to mark the place called Sumaeres Forda which is a reference point on a charter dated 909. The other is the farm called Oxenford Grange, which stands within sight of the great house of Peper Harow. The farm stands on historic ground, since this was probably the two acres granted in 1123 to Waverley Abbey, and it is a local tradition that it served as a granary for the abbey. The present house is possibly late seventeenth century. In front of it is a massive barn built on utilitarian medieval lines, but only about a century ago, by Pugin, and behind the house is a fragment, it seems, of a medieval monastery, but this was built at the same time as the barn. The whole congeries of follies was put up by order of the then Lord Middleton to give an atmosphere of historicity to his outlook from Peper Harow which is part of the parish of Shackleford now.

This tiny village lies just to the west of A3. Many of the houses are old but the church was built by 1865 by Sir Gilbert Scott.

There are five parts to the parish of Shackleford: Shackleford itself, Norney, Eashing, Hurtmore and Peper Harow, though the latter has its own church. It could be said that there are also five distinct worlds in this Shackleford parish: in Shackleford itself there are cottagers, some of whom are employed in a big local market garden whose proprietors also own the attractive cricket ground nearly opposite Mulberry House which was once the rectory. Norney's population is largely made up by commuters, who, in some instances, have bought and reconstructed cottages. In Hurtmore there are council estates for factory workers and Peper Harow is to some extent dominated by the big mansion, Park House. This was the seat of Lord Middleton; there had been a large house on this site since the fourteenth century but the present building was built in 1760; its handsome lines have been somewhat spoiled by the addition of a top storey in 1913 so that the stables, also designed by Chambers, are now more noteworthy from the architectural point of view. In 1942, Lord Middleton died at the age of 86; he had been a member of the Conservative ministry at the beginning of this century and his house had been frequently visited by Curzon, Balfour, the young Winston Churchill and other political notabilities. The estate, however, was broken up on the death of this Lord Middleton and in 1951 his house became an approved school, the stables being converted into workshops. There is a delightful cricket ground opposite the mansion and football pitches are also available for the boys.

Before the last war, the Middletons were dominant in Peper Harow which they ruled with benevolent autocracy. As in Victorian times, the tenants were expected to attend church every Sunday and unexplained absence would invariably be the subject of critical comment from Lord Middleton! There were three other aristocrats who wielded great influence in the parish of Shackleford in pre-

A row of cottages at Ewhurst

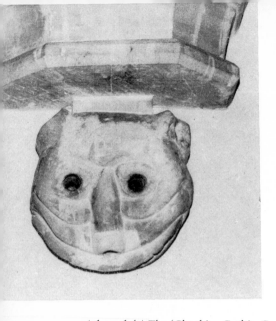

(*above left*) The 'Cheshire Cat' in Cranleigh Church
(*above right*) A window heading in Frensham Church

Fifteenth-century church hall and church, Alfold

The Jacobean pulpit in Alfold Church

The Crown Inn, Chiddingfold

Cottages at Dunsfold

war days, Sir Edgar Horne, the owner of the Hall Place, being one of them. This house was built in 1738 but was completely rebuilt in 1900; it is now a preparatory school. At Eashing, Lord Antrim held sway and there was also Lady Grenville in the Norney area. Today, there are large-scale farmers who have bought land from the huge estates when they broke up under the pressure of wars and death duties; it was when they broke up also that the farm cottages were sold for as little as £600 or £700, a laughable figure compared with their prices today.

Peper Harow church has been heavily restored but it is very attractive from the outside. Almost opposite it is a farm which has an enormous early seventeenth-century granary which stands upon stilts and there are barns and byres also of gargantuan proportions. The farmyard is a most magnificent sight, with an element of the picturesque introduced by a group of cottages which look like chicks nestling under the wing of the granary and other main buildings. This granary alone makes a visit to Peper Harow worth while, but the hamlet is altogether delightful.

The tiny hamlet of Eashing lies on the other side of the A3 from its parent parish of Shackleford.

One of the six water-mills listed as existing in Surrey in the Domesday record must surely have been that at Eashing. It is unfortunate that the building now standing there in its place is an unpleasantly strident affair, because the hamlet itself is charming, if you can accept, as you must in these days, that lucre has preserved it as a weekend retreat for the wealthy.

The bridge is immensely old, and looks it. History tells us that great floods struck this part of the country in 1233, and that some six bridges were built around here as a result of them. Eashing was one of these. The great rugged buttresses still split the waters and the old brick and stone rear nobly up to the road. There is no railing. Breathalyzers were not needed in the thirteenth century; the river saw off the drunken driver! The bridge and the fine row of cottages beyond, probably built not too long after it, are now protected by the National Trust.

Behind the enormity of the mill stands the 'Stag' public-house, another basically splendid building spoiled by too much publicans' mock medieval and suburban facetiousness. The group of houses

K

to the north of the river make an appealing picture and should be seen.

Of Milford no one has a good word to say. Even Ogilvy, writing in 1914, found "not a great deal of interest at Milford", and Eric Parker has said that "on a summer Saturday" it "is less a village than a road". Almost truer would be to say that it is a series of traffic-lights and one large roundabout from which roads radiate in every direction. One of these, the Petworth road, runs through the attractive village of Witley, which can be left to bring this chapter to a worthy end.

One of the historical 'facts' we all know is that the Duke of Clarence was drowned in a butt of Malmsey wine. What we do not know is that this foul deed, if local legend can be believed, took place at Witley. Domesday records Witley as belonging to Richer de l'Aigle, who had inherited it from his father, who had been awarded it by the Conqueror after Hastings. One Earl Godwin had held it before. The Aigle family, or Aquila or Eagle, lost it in 1235 when one of the descendants went back to Normandy without the King's permission. Then it became a royal manor and the manor house, which stood just behind the present church, became a hunting-lodge, a useful overnight stop as well between the coast and London. Legend has it that the ill-fated Duke of Clarence met his end here.

This is one of the oldest churches in the county, though the inevitable accretions of the centuries have overloaded its ancient simplicity; Victorian glass diminishes the beauty of the thirteenth-century windows, even of the tiny Norman windows that peep out here and there; the chancel is a permanent memorial to our forebears' bad taste, and pre-Raphaelite perfection vies with moral messages on floor and ceiling. All this is the relic of the restoration of 1889 which added a wooden ceiling to the tower and to the nave, and which built most of the north aisle. It is high time the Church Council showed the courage and good sense required to remove the clutter of that unfortunate age and turned this lovely building into the glorious creation it was meant to be, as has been done at Shere, or Pyrford.

The existence of a church here is noted in Domesday, and some elements of the present building clearly date from the late Norman period, notably the tall arched doorway into the church, through the modern porchway, and the small windows at the side of the south transept and the section of round-headed window in the south wall of the nave. The timber-work of the two small transepts' roofs probably date from this period as well, and the carved string-course in wood at the top of the north transept's wall is an extremely rare example of such work.

The tower, massive and squat, is thought to be of the thirteenth century, though the pinnacles and the stone balustrade are somewhat later, later even than the spire. Certainly the arches below it that form the crossing in the church are of that period. It was then that the chancel was extended to its present shape from what had probably been a small apse shut away by a narrow Norman arch. The manor chapel would have been built then as well. This retained its lancet windows, while the main east window, possibly altered again later, has the characteristics of the Decorated style of the second half of the fourteenth century. The aumbry and attractive piscina beside the altar are probably of the same era.

On the south wall of the nave is an intriguing wall painting, especially intriguing in that it offers the amateur equal terms with the expert; nothing much is certain about it, and anyone can determine for himself the date, the style and the subject-matter of it. The series of scenes, fairly obviously from the New Testament, are painted boldly in sepia in a style reminiscent of Byzantine work. Many of the figures are very clear and seem to have been drawn in something like the modern strip cartoonist's manner, simple, forthright, straightforward. It is what they are doing that remains to be defined. Our belief, which seems to coincide mostly with that of the Vicar but not with that of the late Professor Tristam, is that the series tells the story of the Nativity, with the Annunciation in the embrasure of the little Norman part-window, and moving to the shepherds in the middle of the top line, through the worship of the Magi at the bottom left and the adoration of Heaven and Earth at bottom right. And the date? Your guess again! The paint lies on Saxon plaster, but the Byzantine simplification seems to point to the twelfth century.

We cannot leave Witley church without recalling the unhappy affair of 1544 when the 'lewd and naughty' curate of the village was summoned before no less a body than the Privy Council in London because he had 'used words'. What the words were remains, perhaps fortunately, wrapped in mystery, but the 1540s were a time of considerable religious uncertainty and confusion in England, with Henry VIII apparently swaying between orthodox Catholic doctrines and the new Protestant ideas, so it is probable that the curate's words were of a theological nature, unless they were tactless comments upon the king's numerous marital adventures.

Originally Witley was almost certainly an agricultural community surrounded by vast woodlands, placed, as it is, mainly on the Bargate Beds of the Greensand. By the sixteenth century, however, it had become set in ways of prosperity; ironstone deposits had led to the creation of a flourishing smelting trade, and woollen cloth was processed in cottages, having been cleaned and beaten in fulling mills established near the plentiful water supply by the Enton Ponds. The presence of water was essential to both these industries, as it was, of course, to the great mill that served the district by Great Enton water, of which the lovely house there now bears witness. Beside all this, the timber provided the charcoal for fuelling the industries and was exported also to the Chiddingfold's glassworks and maybe even further afield to the gunpowder factories at Chilworth. The great number of Elizabethan and Stuart houses in the neighbourhood, so popular now with wealthy commuters, is a reminder of the period of Witley's heyday. On the Godalming side of Witley can be seen one particularly fine example of these, The Old Manor. This was once owned by a tenant farmer of Milford Manor and it has a lovely garden. The house is in two distinct parts, the latest of which dates from the eighteenth century and has the windows typical of that attractive period. The front door, though it gives access to the older part of the house, is in Adam style.

The sitting-room has a most unusual rounded chimney, the lower part of which is completely visible, while the dining-room has an equally handsome and interesting brick chimney cowl. The plaster in this room conceals aged brickwork. The main stairs have planks of fine elm. This handsome house has been suitably furnished by its present owners, Mr. and Mrs. G. Bayley; among their pictures is a large and decorative Hoppner. The manor house was once a hotel and the barn near to it was then used as a dining- and reception-room, by the hotel owner. Now the barn has been skilfully converted into two houses, extremely striking from the outside because of their black and white timbering and, in the case of one of them at least, equally striking inside for the discreet usage of modern appurtenances in old settings.

There are many fine old cottages in the centre of the village and this also has, close to the church, a splendid inn, 'The White Hart'; this has been a public house for well over 200 years and the building itself is considerably older. George Eliot, the Victorian novelist, is supposed to have used an inglenook seat there as a convenient writing-place, though quite why she should have left her comfortable home in order to write in a public-house has not been explained. Witley during the latter part of the nineteenth century was the abode of many writers and artists who were held in high regard at the time but are now merely names.

8

The Weald 1

VERY few manors existed in the Weald forest at the time of Domesday. Communities did, however, in the course of time, grow up in the midst of that daunting and unproductive land. Whether they sprang up as a result of an expression of individualism by break-away groups, a flight to freedom by renegade bondmen, or whether they began as a legally constituted community originally owing feudal service, but becoming more independent because of difficulties of communication, is unsure.

The very name of Charlwood is held to mean the 'wood of the free churls (ceorls)'. The earliest record of the place shows it to have been part of the Manor of Merstham, held by the prior and convent of Christchurch, and in 1231 the prior was writing in some humility to his 'freemen of Cherlewood' seeking their assistance in paying off certain debts. This hardly seems the style of a feudal lord writing to entirely subservient vassals.

Today the parish is mainly agricultural and, apart from the limestone heights that run to the west from Russ Hill through to Stanhill, is set in the heavy Weald clay. In its heyday, however, there were several ironworks, and Charlewood enjoyed an exemption from an Act of Elizabeth I that prohibited the cutting down of trees above a certain size. The working of iron required plentiful wood for the charcoal and water to work the hammers, as well as ironstone from which the metal was extracted. All these were present here. The only memorials of that industry still to be found are in the so-called Forge Cottage in the village and the splendid curved hinge on the massive door of the church.

The church is magnificent, largely because it has almost entirely escaped the attentions of the earnest restorers of the last century. Certainly cement has been inserted, sometimes roughly, here and there, but mostly the medieval work has been left untouched.

Originally this was a compact early Norman building, a solid rectangular nave divided from what was, probably, an apse by a heavy, square tower. To this was added, towards the end of the thirteenth century, a south aisle, somewhat narrower than the nave. About the same time the Norman apse was replaced by a large, square-ended chancel. The final addition was an extension eastwards of the south aisle to form a chapel to the memory of Richard Saunders, or Sanders, of Sanders Place, in 1480—this is the present chancel—and the building of a small porch to the south doorway. It may be that the top of the tower was rebuilt at the same time. Since then the fabric has largely been left undisturbed.

The Norman nave remains. Some of the great sandstone quoins of that construction are still to be seen on the outside of the western and north-western corners, and a tiny round-headed window is still deeply recessed in the north wall. The arches on each side of the tower are of well-preserved Norman style, simple semicircular heads with typical zigzag moulding. The thirteenth-century chancel beyond the tower is now the vestry.

The chancel is separated from the body of the church by a beautiful wooden screen of the same age as the chapel itself (1480), with double doors made to close the central opening—a parclose door. From a row of solid, plain panels along the bottom spring shapely columns to support, with pointed arches, the ornate cornice of a design of vine leaves and bunches of grapes. Above this is a decoration moulded in gesso made out of repeated initials, R.S. (for Richard Saunders), supported by winged dragons. Over the opening are panels with the Saunders and Carew arms and the monogram IHS and a crowned M, for the Virgin Mary, all held up by angels. Careful recent redecoration has brought out the brilliance of this work of art.

This is not the end of the interest of this church; along the south wall is a large area of medieval painting. Some of it, that on the eastern side of the window, represents the unhappy adventures of St. Margaret. She, poor girl, was being nurtured in innocence near Antioch, when she caught the fancy of the High Sheriff of the land, one Olibrius, who had her seized by his men. When she refused his advances she was beaten, imprisoned and then, still holding firm, fed to a dragon. Such was her power that the dragon burst and she stepped out unharmed. This was not enough, however, and she was finally beheaded. This story, painted in fresco, at the time of the building in 1280, is told visually here. On the other side of the window are two stories, the product clearly of different times and intermingled, the one of an incident from the life of St. Nicholas, and the other a popular morality. The morality concerns three wealthy young men out hunting who came up against the gruesome sight of three corpses who warn them of the fate in store for themselves. The large dark figures of the dead dominate the scene and doubtless, in their heyday, struck righteous fear in the hearts of the villagers.

These murals were uncovered from the shrouding whitewash in 1858. When the colours began to fade they were treated with some preservative preparation that greatly accelerated the destructive process. They were carefully restored in 1962.

The pulpit is a fine example of Jacobean carving, the linen-fold design being masterly.

The Saunders family settled in the manor of Charlwood, it seems, in the thirteenth or fourteenth century, and lived in Charlwood Place, once a great, moated mansion. Today, alas, nothing remains, or at least is visible beneath the trappings of highly industrialized agriculture. Charlwood Manor, formerly Taylor's Farm, nearer to the village, is a more striking building, some of it dating from the sixteenth century.

Our own first introduction to the village came many years ago when we played in a very pleasant cricket match on the delightful ground on a fine summer's evening.

The Weald villages are never very close together. Iron-working communities are well separated because of the relative paucity of ore-bearing soils, of course, but also because they needed a good stretch of forest for the charcoal for the furnaces.

Leigh (pronounced Lye) is another 'iron' village and is some $3\frac{1}{2}$ miles as the crow flies from Charlwood. A small tributary of the

Mole, rising on Holmwood Common, flows through the village and certainly provided some of the motive power for the workings. There is a Hammer Bridge, where the Newdigate road crosses the stream. The hamlet of Irons Bottom, to the east, is another relic of the trade. The exemption from Elizabeth's tree-felling Act applied equally to Leigh.

The village-green here is almost perfect, certainly when looked at southwards from the main north-south road. It is a triangular green with the church at the far apex. Along the right-hand edge is the Priests' House, a breathtaking, irregular terrace of basically fifteenth-century buildings, now joined into one excellently restored and cunningly enlarged amalgam of bricks, timber and tiled roofs of differing heights.

Along the left side of the triangle is the village inn, the 'Plough', of which the north wing dates from the fourteenth or fifteenth century. The rest, however, is fairly recent. This is one of a dwindling number of pubs where beer can still be got from the wood, but its décor is unattractive.

The church looks, from the outside, more authentic than in fact it is. Of the original fifteenth-century building, probably dating from the time of John Arderne of Leigh Place, who, in 1432, was High Sheriff of Surrey, little enough remains. It is a little boxlike structure with a square chancel tacked on to the east end, most of it a reconstruction of 1890. Little of the old work was allowed to remain, apart from some interesting memorial brasses.

From 1262, at least, until the dissolution of the monasteries, Leigh parish was held by the prior and convent of Newark Abbey, and the canons took it in turns to officiate, thus saving the cost of paying a resident priest. Perhaps the visits of these worthies are the *raison d'être* of the Priests' House

To the south of the village is Leigh Place, where only a little of the fifteenth-century moated building can be glimpsed amid the reconstruction done in 1810 in the popular romantic Gothick. The great barn is the best part and the square moat is a fine, broad stretch of water. The house itself looks curiously small and insignificant in its setting.

Shellwood Common makes a brief and inglorious entry in the history of the later stages of the Civil War. After the abdication of Richard Cromwell, Oliver's son, the Royalists, taking advantage of the resulting struggle for power, mounted a certain number of rather incompetently managed risings, in one of which a small body of men was heading for Redhill. Commonwealth forces were waiting there for them, however, and they retreated to Shellwood, which they reached on 1st August 1659. Thence, as soon as what would now be called the Security Forces put in an appearance, they fled ignominiously.

The third of the old iron villages of the Weald clay that once formed a closely linked triangle is Newdigate, a pleasant and straggling community now becoming overgrown, being not too far from the railway. The main iron-works were at Ewood, then owned by the Earls of Warenne. The mill dam is still visible as well as the mill itself that has now been turned into a residence.

On the road from there into the village there are some good examples of sixteenth- and seventeenth-century building. The first group of these is formed by the Surrey Oaks Inn, too polished now to be much interest except for refreshments. Opposite are some genuine seventeenth-century cottages. Some similar cottages a little further along have been considerably 'improved'. The effect of urbanization, whether it be for good or for ill, can be seen by a comparison of Reffolds, dating from about 1600, and now more than a little overgrown and dilapidated, and Gaterounds of similar period and smartened up and shining with money well spent.

Other cottages lend an air of colourful authenticity to the village, especially round about the vicinity of the church. Here are Dean House Farm, basically a sixteenth-century brick and timber building that has been strangely chopped short at the side of the road. Opposite the church is the Six Bells Inn with, beside it, two good timbered cottages, White Cottage and Hasted Cottage.

The church itself is an attractive small country structure with a great spread of tiled roof and a shapely shingled tower and spire. This tower is wholly made of wood. In the interior this tower really claims the attention of the visitor since the enormous criss-crossed timbers that carry the weight quite dominate the west end of the building. These great beams must be all of 500 years old.

The restoration of 1876 did little harm to the church. The main period of building must have been just after the end of the Norman age, about 1200, although some elements may well be older. Look, for instance, at the massive round pillar on the south side of the nave. This has incised roughly on it an intricate cross-shaped design that may have some connection with the Knights Templar who had established themselves at the house now called Temple Elfand. The same pillar also has holes in it, possibly the fixing points for the chains that used to prevent removal of the precious newly translated Bible of Henry VIII's age.

Large lancet windows with plain glass stand on either side of the altar and so flood it with light. How fine the chancel would be if the lurid colours of the east window were to be replaced with the cool brilliance of trees, as at Cranleigh, for instance. The chancel is well proportioned and could look imposing with some rehandling now.

There is an unusually shaped squint from the south aisle which has a piscina which shows that it was always intended as a chapel. There is one small brass in the chancel, to Joan, daughter of the late Thomas Smallpiece and late wife of George Steere, parson of this parish, dated 1634. George Steere was rector until 1660 and suffered no trouble, it appears, during the Puritan Government. His must have been a local family and it was to a later relative, in 1775, that Cudworth Manor was sold.

Cudworth lies nearly a mile to the east of Newdigate village, down a dreadful track known as Hog's Pudding Lane. Despite much modernization at various times in its history it is still a fine old building, some of it dating from the thirteenth century. It is surrounded by a broad moat, fed by the neighbouring Mead Brook, and this is crossed by an attractive roofed bridge which contains a dove-cote, all highly romantic. The Manor Farm, nearby, contains a vast and ancient barn, still with its fifteenth-century roof timbers and great tie-beams and king-posts.

There is something mysterious about all these villages that stand as a sort of bulwark before the Sussex border. At one time the great forest must have surrounded them, the more daunting, the more sinister towards the south. Occasional houses stand isolated, hidden from the main roads up rough tracks and behind bastions of age-old trees. Some of these have been rebuilt over the centuries, to become country estates for wealthy families. Others have remained as farms, often now showing the destructiveness of time and the struggle to make ends meet. The farmhouse of Chaffolds, almost on the border, near Rusper, may serve as an example of this. The track to it is appalling and the house is set amid dilapidated outhouses.

It may seem illogical for us to sheer off eastwards again from Newdigate into the furthermost corner of Surrey, but there, too, were some considerable iron-workings. It means crossing the traffic flow of the Brighton road, and now that Gatwick Airport has sealed off some of the few east-west roads, it is almost impossible to avoid the shapeless sprawl of Horley. Industry has spread down the A23 and old Horley has virtually disappeared. To the south of it is Burstow.

Burstow is a scattered village which boasts a twelfth-century church, dedicated to St. Bartholomew. There is, in fact, very little Norman work left in it for there was extensive change in the thirteenth and fifteenth century while, quite recently, there has been a laudable attempt to brighten the interior at some cost to the atmosphere of antiquity that such an ancient church should have. The tower and spire were restored in 1902 but mercifully retain the timber of the former and the shingles of the latter so that Burstow can still boast of its timber tower. There is a magnificent peal of bells and the ringing chamber, also timbered, is a fascinating place. The atmosphere of the ringing chamber is further assisted by the presence of an old wooden chest of the Tudor period.

The most notable feature of the church interior is the two niches, one on each side of the chancel arch, though, of course, the saints or holy figures that once occupied them did not survive the Puritan ravages—or perhaps the no less serious ravages of Henry VIII's campaign against 'superstition'. The first rector named on the board began his cure in 1294; between 1637 and 1684 a certain Cooke held the living, apparently without interruption, suggesting that, like the Vicar of Bray, he found no difficulty in conforming to the various changes that took place in the country's religion in the mid-century. An unusual memorial spans the altar and commemorates John Flamsteed, rector from 1684 until 1719 and also the first man to be appointed Astronomer Royal; the interest always shown by Charles II in scientific matters is attested by this interesting appointment. On the north of the altar is a curious recess which might well have been an aumbry.

In the course of the fifteenth-century alterations, changes were made in the windows, possibly on the instructions of Archbishop Chichele, whose coat of arms, adorning one of these windows, was, according to legend, taken out by the *nouveau riche* owner of Smallfield Place, Bysshe, and replaced by his own. No Bysshe arms survive in the present windows so the truth of the story cannot be ascertained—but it is in keeping with the known facts of Bysshe's life.

Next door to the church is a fine house, Old Court, of the late seventeenth or early eighteenth century, and not far from the church is Burstow Court, which has a moat and some sixteenth-century portions. Apart from these, Burstow is an undistinguished village which appears to lack a centre.

Smallfield is rather a dreary little village, and lies within the purview of Burstow. There is a Bysshe Place there, as well as a lovely Tudor house, now divided into two and previously called either Smallfield Place or Crullings, as its history relates.

In medieval times, land here was held by a certain Crulling, and it seems that the fine fifteenth-century manor house called Crullings took its name from this family. When the house was restored early in the seventeenth century by Sir Edward Bysshe into whose possession it had just come, he renamed it Smallfield Place as he did not think that Crullings was a sufficiently grand title. Now the house has been skilfully divided into two parts, one of which is called Crullings and the other Smallfield Place. This Solomonic judgment has, it is hoped, appeased the ghosts of its two earlier owners.

There are a number of attractive though improbable legends connected with this house, one being that it was granted to a certain John de Burstow by Edward III after the latter had had an accident while riding; another that Henry VIII used it as a lodge for stag-hunting and once chased a stag as far as Walton; another again that Anne Boleyn wrote a letter from it, though to whom, about what and when remains wrapped in mystery. Certainty comes, however, with the purchase of the house by Bysshe in 1613; he died in 1655 and was succeeded in ownership of Smallfield Place by his son who was an M.P. and also became Garter King of Arms in the period of the Civil War, Commonwealth and Protectorate.

M.P. for Reigate in 1654, Sir Edward managed to keep well in the swim when Charles II was restored in 1660. During the Commonwealth, Bysshe had done his utmost—with some success—to preserve the valuable heralds' library and so, though he ceased to be Garter King of Arms in 1660, he secured instead the post of Clarenceux herald. That invaluable retailer of gossip John Aubrey characteristically describes Sir Edward as "active in the iniquity of the times, ate the bread of loyalists and accepted a pension of £600 p.a. from sequestrators".

Pension or no, Sir Edward soon found himself in financial difficulties after the Restoration and began to use his office to amend his fortunes with disastrous results; bankrupt, he was forced to abandon his house and in 1679 died in poverty in Covent Garden.

Of the two houses today, Smallfield Place has a fine front, Crullings a magnificent staircase, a beautiful fireplace and bow-window in the drawing-room and a priests' hole, the latter suggesting that at some time in the late sixteenth or early seventeenth century the owner was a Catholic who gave shelter to one of the itinerant priests who at that time sought, not without success, to keep the flame of Rome still burning.

The loveliest village in eastern Surrey, and certainly the largest, is Lingfield, a place to linger in, and we make no apology for so doing.

Where the higher backbone of the Weald lay stretched out from east to west across the middle of southern England, the action of weather and streams slowly ate away the thick and heavy clay crust and floated it down to the lower regions. Underneath lay a sort of Sachertorte of layers of sandstone and Hastings clays. Here and there these reach the surface and provide, perhaps, a more fertile subsoil. Odd outcrops are to be seen at Outwood and near Charlwood and Leigh. A bigger area is found round Lingfield, where orchards and hopfields once provided the agricultural wealth where the circumstances did not create a rather barren, heath area as on Dry Hill, on which were suitable conditions for an Iron Age fort against the invasions that swept in from Kent.

Lingfield today is a large village with nearly 7,000 inhabitants and a number of country roads converge on it. It was, no doubt, once a considerable market. It had a mineral spring which Aubrey visited, but he seems to have enjoyed the local ale more than the waters. There was flourishing iron industry here in the sixteenth century and the sixteen large guns mysteriously owned by Sir Thomas Cawarden of Blechingley may have been made here. The Surrey iron industry survived various vicissitudes until the eighteenth century and then declined entirely because the iron-master unpatriotically supplied guns to France when that country was at war with Britain and the government in 1779 transferred its contracts to Scotland. These ironworks also operated just across the Kent border at Scarlets and Cowden, and an off-shoot, a bloomery or wrought-iron works, existed at 'The Beeches', just on the Surrey side of the border.

One of the greatest of the local families in medieval England to arise from this neighbourhood was that of the Cobhams who lived at Starborough Castle, some 3 miles to the east of the village. Their great house has almost completely disappeared, the last depredations being those perpetrated only recently when for a short time it was a private hotel, the first in 1649 by order of Parliament which feared that it might become a rallying point for royalists.

The family is well remembered in the church which they re-fashioned and enlarged in the fourteenth century, building a lofty north aisle and the chancel in which they now lie in their magnificent tombs. The first Lord Cobham's tomb is on the south side of the north chapel; his effigy shows a tough fighter and general and his head rests on a helmet with a Saracen's head to show his descent from a crusader. This Cobham fought at Crécy and later held many important posts which made him one of the great men of the realm. He died of plague in 1361.

His son had ordered that he should be buried at the rear of his father's head, so perhaps his tomb was moved from there to its present position against the north wall at a later date. His tomb brass is so fine that rubbing it is wisely prohibited. His life was eventful: exiled by Richard II after being one of the commissioners appointed to rule during the king's minority, he met Henry Bolingbroke in Brittany and returned with him to overthrow Richard, dying four years later in 1403. His Latin epitaph salutes him as "brave as a leopard, sumptuous in his housekeeping, handsome, affable, munificent and generous".

The third Lord Cobham and his wife lie in front of the high altar. It was he who founded the Carthusian College which took over the church as its place of worship in 1431 and he rebuilt the church, except for the tower, in the same year. His tomb is magnificent, the two marble figures being in excellent condition. Its sides are decorated with family coats of arms. This Lord Cobham fought at Agincourt and died in 1446. Twenty-five years later this family, which had had so many notable aristocratic connections (including Roger Mortimer, executed by Edward III in 1330), died out.

The memorial brasses on the floor beside the tombs include those of a nameless lady whose costume is precisely etched, a smaller outline of Isabella Cobham, one of Eleanor, first wife of the third Lord Cobham, and one of Katherine Stockete, lady-in-waiting to the wife of the first Lord Cobham to whom she bequeathed £30.

In the nave of the north aisle is another fine brass, covered with a carpet, which depicts a knight in full armour; his name is hard to read but his coat of arms is that of the Sondes family who held Puttenden Manor after 1477. On the north wall nearby is a large plaque to Sir James Burrow of Starborough Castle, twice President of the Royal Society, who died in 1782. Reference is made to his convivial character. Nearer the east end of this wall are two tall clay plaques bearing the figures of gentlemen praying. There are traces of golden umber glaze but the plaques are in poor condition; they may have come originally from the college buildings.

This almost completes the list of memorials but three more are noteworthy. One of these may especially interest Americans; it is a large, formal slab to Charles and Philadelphia Howard, son and daughter of Francis, Lord Howard of Effingham and his wife Philadelphia who died in 1684. Perhaps William Penn, founding

Pennsylvania, named its capital after one of these Howard ladies. Not far from this is another slab, part of whose inscription carries the command:

> Desist those prophane feet, forebeare,
> To fowle this Hallowed Marbles, where
> Lies vertues, Goodnes, honours heire.

Lastly, there is William Widnell (?) of whom it is said:

> 'Cause the world was not worthy him to have
> The great Jehovah shutt him in this grave,

an event that occurred in 1662.

This is a fine church despite the Victorian glass in most of the fifteenth-century windows. The nave and the north aisle, which is almost as large as the nave, are spacious and lofty, roofed with an arch-braced wooden ceiling which is, unusually, completely boarded in. The north and south chapels are cut off by magnificent parclose screens, patched but authentic and probably dating from 1431.

The main chancel is enclosed by the stalls of the members of the college, some of which are back to the congregation and several of which have misericords, expertly carved. The south window of the sanctuary has some pieces of medieval glass inserted in jig-saw style and containing coats of arms. The font is Tudor stone-work with quatrefoil designs each with a rose in its centre: in two of the roses a human face may be discerned. The wooden cover has gilded and painted crockets.

The tower is the oldest part of the building and was untouched in the fifteenth-century reconstruction. It is a great, sturdy, but-tressed square, surmounted by a balustrade with cusped decora-tions and by a small, shingled spire. The south door shows the remains of a large arch, suggesting that it was once an impressive portico; the smaller doorway was inserted into the old framework. Inside, the present archway is set in what looks as if it were a round-headed Norman arch.

The stone turret against the outside north wall may have once served as a beacon to guide wanderers across the land between the church and the Kentish border, but as it is similar to structures found in monastic refectories to enable the reader to reach his

L

place, it is much more likely to have housed the stairway to the
rood-loft. It certainly adds another element of interest to this
superb church whose splendour has not been too much diminished
by restorations in the last century. It gains by being surrounded
by fascinating houses, some of which, on the south side of the
church, were until quite recently village shops. One was once the
Star Inn and is now the Church House (an interesting transformation!), while Pollard House, considerably older, was a butcher's
shop. Nearer the church on the same side as Church House is
Church Gate Cottage, a beautiful sixteenth-century building
formerly a sweet shop. Opposite the west door of the church is an
early Georgian farmhouse, now in a decrepit state but possibly
soon to be rescued by careful restoration.

The guest house which once entertained visitors to the college is
on the north side of the church; built in the fifteenth century it
was well restored in 1897 and then given to the village by the
restorer's son. Part of it now houses the public library in which
the unusual roof with original crossbeams is noteworthy, as is the
mechanical spit, operated by rope and weight, in the fireplace of the
junior library. This is thought to be one of three now existing in
Surrey.

J. S. Ogilvy had an interesting experience when sketching the
old houses near the church just before the Great War. Lingfield
by then had an important racecourse, constructed for National
Hunt meetings in 1890 and extended for flat races four years
later. Ogilvy's visit coincided with a meeting and he records that
the village was full of men in faded hunting costume whom he
rather naïvely took to be "some kind of officials on duty round
the public-houses". They were in fact racecourse touts who later
in the morning benefited in a curious way from the artist's
presence: "My position at the roadside became rather uncom-
fortable, and when tubby men in sporting clothes began to throw
pennies at me in the belief that I was a racecourse freak, it
was time to quit, rather to the disappointment of my scarlet-
coated friends for whom I had provided a sort of nucleus and
who looked after all the stray pennies in a way that occasionally
resembled a football scrimmage." Inspired by this anecdote, our
photographer spent a considerable time taking the old houses,

but to his disappointment no horsey gentlemen showered him with coins.

Lingfield once had two names, Plaistow Street being the area round the old oak tree and the village cage half a mile from the church. St. Peter's Cross once stood near the tree and legend once said that on the top of it was a basin to catch rain for use as holy water. In 1891 doubt was cast upon this tale though the suggestion was then made that the cross might have been erected in 1431 when the college was founded. No trace of it remains today.

The village cage or lock-up was almost certainly built in 1773 and was used to incarcerate poachers as late as 1882. A glimpse into its gloomy interior suggests that law-breakers were either very few in number or very small in stature. Near it is the huge oak now propped up with metal supports and this, with the cage and the ornamental pond, makes an attractive central area of the village. There are cottages with Horsham slab roofs, the Old Cage restaurant (early sixteenth with clever modern additions) and the handsome Greyhound Inn to complete the picture. In Station Road there is the fine New Place, built in 1617 with an impressive main entrance and a good staircase. Also in this road are two pleasant cottages, side by side, called Tally-Ho and Hunter's End.

On Lingfield's outskirts is Puttenden Manor, the main portion of which was built in 1477 (this is the part on the left of a visitor who is facing the main entrance); the middle portion was built in 1674 and the right-hand part in 1905 by the Napier family who then owned the house.

Puttenden today is lived in and can be visited on certain days in summer. An opportunity is thus offered to see a largely fifteenth-century house which is not just a museum. Some of the furnishings are out of period and lack artistic merit but the house makes a fine impression; we like the kitchen with its array of implements, the dining-room with its huge table, and the priest's hole which tells us that one of the Sondes family must have adhered to the Catholic faith during the sixteenth- and seventeenth-century persecution. The gallery has a more modern interest because leading Liberal politicians used to meet there early in this century as did prominent men of letters and art in the late Victorian period. The present owner, Mr. Brian Donovan Thompson, is to be thanked for the care with which he has looked after this splendid manor.

This part of Surrey is rich in old houses, for near Puttenden is Old Surrey Hall, a moated house with an interesting history. Until recently this was simply the hall of what had been a big Tudor house. A farmer lived in this and had partitioned it to form several rooms, and his wife was once visited by a number of learned gentlemen who sought permission to inspect the hall and to hear a lecture on it from one of their number. The wife willingly gave permission and was somewhat dismayed to find that she was excluded from the meeting!

It may have been built by the Gaynesfords in 1450 and it changed hands frequently until it became a farmhouse. In the 1920s it was restored and extended, the new wings being very skilful imitations of the Tudor style.

The last great house of the Tudor period in this neighbourhood is Crowhurst Place, a timbered house with a moat and a lovely garden which was once owned by the Marlborough family. Crowhurst village church has a good spire, a fine old parish chest and a good font but it has suffered from restoration. Even the yew tree in the churchyard had a door cut into it and a seat placed inside it by a publican in 1820.

The scattered village of Outwood probably owes its existence to the small area of sandstone, sticking up like an island on which it stands. The name suggests a separate outlying community in, or at the edge of, the wood. The sandstone may well have made it a more profitable agricultural district than the rest of the clay forest.

The present community, where it has not become pure commuterdom, is still agricultural. It is set in beautiful country, and country that is virtually safe from spoilation owing to the generous gifts in 1955 and 1959 by Mr. and Mrs. T. H. Lloyd of the whole of the Harewoods Estate, which contains much of Outwood, to the National Trust. There are one or two fine Georgian houses there, as well as the oldest working mill in the country, a smock mill of 1665. To say it is a 'working' mill requires some qualification; the machinery does indeed work still, but the mill no longer grinds corn. It is a show-piece, and the owner has added a little menagerie and a rustic museum for the entertainment of visitors.

The church is disappointing. From the outside the Victorian building looks pleasantly and modestly unpretentious but inside it has something of the appearance of a red-brick army drill-hall on a small scale. This is sad, because the setting is a fine one, and Outwood is lucky enough to possess one of the loveliest cricket grounds in the county tucked away among trees down a lane. The game there is old-fashioned and sporting, and sixes send the players scurrying into the forest to find the ball, and it is all quite delightful.

9

The Weald 2

ON the western side of the greensand, hills stretch further southwards and press the Weald clay into a narrower strip. The ancient forest was here, doubtless, as impenetrable as it was to the east, but here, at least, the Romans pierced it with the earliest and the greatest of their north-south roads, Stane Street. Though some iron was worked in this district, there was a wider range of industrial activity, brickworks and glass-making, for example.

The road south from Dorking does not follow the old Roman line. It skirts the greensand hills and the Holmwoods and Beare Green stretch out in characterless ribbons along it.

Further south is Capel. It is to be hoped that one day the road may be made to by-pass it and thus spare this village the present very heavy flow of traffic.

The name Capel derives, quite simply, from chapel, for this was once part of Dorking parish then called Dorking *cum Capella*. This part of the county, right down to the Sussex border, was more noted for its pigs than for its human population—and there is no mention of Capel in Domesday Book. At some time in the twelfth century, however, the chapel was built and a village sprang up which was then called Ewekene. In 1282, Henry de Ewekene was in charge of the church; apparently it is not known when it changed its patron saint from St. Lawrence to the present saint, John the Baptist and it is not known when it broke away from Dorking. There is, however, one definite and interesting piece of information about it in the mid-seventeenth century when the vicar, John Allen, was ejected by the Puritans because he had, *inter alia*, invented a cure for toothache. The holder of the tithes was ordered to provide the stipend of his replacement but adamantly refused to do so and the church was left without a minister until the plunder obtained from the Chapter of Winchester was partly employed for this purpose.

Today, St. John the Baptist is a fine specimen of a village church despite the inevitable restoration in 1865. A magnificent yew tree spreads itself lavishly in the churchyard, the wooden tower and oak-shingled spire, of a type very commonly found in the Wealden churches, are both handsome and the west porch has very unusual semi-circular rafters. This is original and is not the only thirteenth-century feature of the church: the roof, the south and west doors with dog-tooth mouldings, the stone buttress at the south-east corner of the nave and the piscina on the south wall of the chancel have all survived. There is also a monument to an Elizabethan lawyer, John Cowper, who was "sergeant at the law, in which degree he contynued one yeare and a haulfee and then ended his life on the 15th daye of Marche 1590". Obviously much more recent than these features are the gaily painted organ pipes in the north aisle which bring a touch of the fairground into the church, the ugly stone pulpit which replaced a wooden one in 1865 and the lich-gate of the same period.

In Capel itself there are two inns, the 'King's Head' and the 'Crown', of some antiquity, some attractive old cottages and three notable houses. First among these is Temple Elfand which derives its name from the Knights Templar who are supposed to have built it. This house has had an interesting history in more recent times, being used for some years as a place for training guard-dogs. There are good outbuildings, a very deep and aged well, and ponds (possibly once the monks' stewponds) and an extremely handsome paddock wall. The house itself has Tudor beams in one section.

There are two other grand houses in Capel, on the Rusper road. One is called Taylor's Farm and dates from the fifteenth and sixteenth centuries. It is no longer a farm but is divided into three separate dwellings; the outbuildings are in some decay; they include a curious structure which resembles a bus-stop shelter and which contains a mural of Far Eastern scenes. Not far away is

the really magnificent Ridge Farm which is also fifteenth and
sixteenth century and has remarkable crooked black door posts
and a barn skilfully modernized into a cottage. The preservation
of the house and outbuildings and the obvious care lavished upon
the garden are much to the credit of the owner, Mr. Arthur Rowe.
William Cobbett once wrote "when the old farmhouses are down
(and down they must come in time) what a miserable thing the
country will be". Cobbett was not to know that many fine old
farmhouses would survive because, in the twentieth century, there
were people with sufficient taste and sufficient means to preserve
them.

Westwards from Capel three villages are strung out in a line
just under the greensand hills. Almost certainly their early settlement came because of their proximity to the primitive civilization
that kept, for defensive purposes as well, perhaps, as for comfort,
to the higher lands. These three villages are Ockley, Ewhurst and
Cranleigh.

Of the numerous lovely village greens in Surrey, Ockley's must
have some claim to be considered the most beautiful. Its setting
is quite splendid with the Downs away to the north making a
superb backcloth; around the green itself are a number of fine old
cottages, and village cricket at its very best has been played on the
pitch in the middle of it for many years. On Stane Street is 'The
Cricketers' and The Red Lion Inn, both seventeenth-century inns,
though the noises emanating from a juke-box in the latter when
we visited it recently were all too horribly twentieth century. There
should be a society to fight a campaign against the prevalent habit
of making people take their meals to the accompaniment of totally
unnecessary music—as if good conversation were not the proper
corollary of good food.

Ockley's charm extends to its houses and cottages; Carpoles on
Stane Street and the two cottages named after this house and
situated on the edge of the green are particularly noteworthy; on
the left-hand side of Stane Street going south there is an old cottage which seems to be falling into decay, in marked contrast to
one almost opposite it which has obviously been recently restored:
to be more accurate, it has had a 'facelift' while its identical neighbour remains unadorned, the whole rather resembling one of those

advertisements for 'before' and 'after'. Tucked away in one corner of the green is a small church built in the late nineteenth century, no doubt in order to provide a more central place of worship than the parish church which is quite a considerable distance east of the main part of the village. The parish church has many handsome features which have survived the restoration of 1873. The nave roof, for example, has early fourteenth-century moulded tie-beams and plates, and the south wall of the nave with its doorway and windows is of the same period. The marble chancel is a memorial to a 19-year-old lieutenant who was killed at the first battle of Ypres in 1914—yet another tragic reminder of the terrible casualties sustained in the Great War. Less sad—and far less common —are the memorial tablets high on the west wall to the churchwardens who were in office in 1700 when the six bells were hung and the tower was rebuilt. In the bell chamber is a fine chest of which no doubt these churchwardens and their predecessors once had the keys.

The date of the first rector given on the list of incumbents is 1308 and the red and gold glass which adorns the window just east of the porch is thought to be a few years after 1308.

Aubrey writes of a custom prevalent at Ockley whereby a red rose tree was planted over the graves of lovers who died before marriage; but there are no rose trees in the graveyard now, so either the custom has completely died out or else Aubrey was confusing Ockley with Ockham.

In 851 the Danes were defeated in a great battle by King Ethelwulf and his Saxons and it may be that Ockley was the scene of this battle; the brook bordering the green was said to have run with blood after the great slaughter of the Danish invaders. It cannot be confidently asserted that this was the location of this famous battle but Mr. Ogilvy states that the villagers still talked about it; he was writing just before the Great War began, which no doubt gave the people of the village often unhappier subjects of conversation about war and battles. There was also a castle at Ockley, near the parish church. It was built by the Clares during the turbulent reign of Stephen (1135–1154) but demolished by his successor, Henry II. Even earlier than the castle, of which only the motte now survives, was Almar's Mill, so called after the owner of the farm on which it stood whose tenure is mentioned in Domesday Book.

Ewhurst never seems to get the fair crack of the whip it deserves from those who write, or wrote, about Surrey. Mostly it has only a passing mention, perhaps because a large part of the church was rebuilt in 1837 as a result of a misfortune when workmen were underpinning the central tower and, by some inefficient calculation, let it drop, destroying much of the chancel and the north transept. In fact the reconstruction was well done under the direction of Robert Ebbels and the church stands proudly and picturesquely on a small hillock with some attractive houses at its gates. One of these was an inn, 'The Bull', until fairly recently. Indeed it was here that Cobbett, in 1823, "treated my horse to some oats, and myself to a rasher of bacon", before pressing on, in spite of warnings about the dreadful state of the road, to Ockley. The house later became the post office, but is now a private house. On the other side of the church entrance is a much prettified cottage, now with delicate bow-windows.

A comparison with the extent of neighbouring parishes, which show reasonably enough that the early settlements extended well south into the clay of the Weald, suggests that Ewhurst at one time grew enough in importance to become divided from Shere and to be established in its own right. Now it sits almost wholly on the clay but extends for a short way on to the greensand hills. The reason for its growth is not completely settled; it may have been the development of ironworks that brought its wealth; it may have been the discovery and utilization of brick-earth, which is still employed today; it may, though this may be only romantic supposition, have been because of its proximity to the old Roman road that ran from Rowhook to Farley Heath and which must have cut close to Ewhurst Green, although no signs of its course have been found here. It is more than likely that this road ran quite close to Old House, which we discovered largely by accident. Our mood was exploratory and we turned down the driveway at the spur of a momentary decision. The drive is long and curls between a thickly growing park. At the end of it, and in a slight hollow, stands this splendidly composed—that is the right word—amalgamation of half-timbered farm buildings. The ancient farm house, quite a small edifice, lies at the back, roofed with the heavy Horsham slabs, and it has been linked most cunningly with the great barn that has been turned into a noble dining-room. The lawns stretch out to the woodland beyond, and the setting is so rustic and medieval that just before our visit the rose gardens had been cleared entirely of blooms by deer.

Ewhurst Green has a few old cottages, but it has also some less attractive modern dwellings lining the open space.

Old Ewhurst—the name means yew wood—straggles up a slight slope that ends in the steep rise up Coneyhurst Hill, and struggles to contain the new houses and the garish signs that are the evidence of the village's continuing growth and popularity, even though it is far from any railway.

The church, despite its reconstruction, is worth a visit. The day we went there, a fine summer afternoon, the present writer was temporarily separated from his co-author when he met the rector coming out. "Three hundred and eight for eight" called the rector. "Not too clever is it?" Co-author would not have been at a loss at this strange greeting; he would have understood the mystic message, England's score in the current Test Match.

The west porch is one of those timber structures that are found here and there in Surrey—at Mickleham, for instance, ancient rafters, and supports now decaying. The former doorway, now blocked, is in the south wall of the nave, and that is a genuine Norman door, though it has been much restored. The shape of the jambs is repeated in the mock Norman of the not unimpressive tower. Inside, the eye is immediately taken by the striking, massive, rough-hewn stonework of the crossing. This gives an interesting focal point and lends an impression of space to the interior. The arches here are of Early English type and there is a clever use of a wider arch on the nave side than on the chancel side, again helping almost by a *trompe-l'oeil* effect to create this sensation of spaciousness. The pulpit is Jacobean and the altar-rails are probably not much more recent. They have twisted supports and are arranged, as in a college chapel, round three sides of the altar. The altar is high-lighted by having two large lancets, one on either side, containing plain glass, thus adding a touch of baroque's dramatic design to a sober English parish church. The south transept is of the thirteenth century and has some old glass coats of arms set in the three good lancets there.

At the northern end of the village is a small group of buildings standing round a tiny green that faces the village inn that presents, unfortunately, a less than attractive façade. The buildings here form a highly picturesque corner, or rather, they would do that were it not for the garish garage and some new building on the northward side.

The third of the present series of villages, Cranleigh, lies rather further south, further from the shelter of the high hills, but on a small tributary of the Wey. It is this, of course, that decided the site for the village.

"It has been developed rather rapidly in recent years and in consequence is suffering from growing pains." These words were not written in 1970, but in 1914, the author being J. S. Ogilvy. What would Mr. Ogilvy have thought of the very recent—and utterly hideous—shopping development in the middle of the village? Certainly in all our perambulations through Surrey we have not encountered anything quite so destructive of the whole concept of what a village should be: these shops would be admirably in place in a 'new' town but their presence in the main street of Cranleigh, a street which still retains a number of handsome old buildings, is an affront to the eyes.

Happily, the visitor to Cranleigh approaching from Guildford has the pleasure of passing the fine cricket field before he reaches the shopping area. This cricket field does not, it must be made clear, provide a pitch for a *village* team, for Cranleigh Cricket Club has a well-deserved reputation among the strongest Surrey club sides, while the wicket and outfield are good enough for Surrey 2nd XI to use. The pavilion *and* its immediate replacement were both burnt down within the space of a few years as a result of arson by someone who obviously disliked cricket. Overlooking the ground are a number of curiously assorted houses, one of which appears to have strayed from a London street of Victorian villas. To counterbalance this, there is the handsome 'Old Tokefield' in timber and plaster, and Pear Tree Cottage which is also attractive though perhaps not so ancient.

Cranleigh cricket should derive some inspiration from the fact that Peter May, former captain of England and of Surrey, has a house bordering the ground, and undoubtedly valuable reinforcements are forthcoming from the masters of Cranleigh School which is only a few hundred yards away from the club ground.

Cranleigh main street is long and, on its left-hand side (coming from Guildford), attractive. At the end of it is the church, next to which is a very old house, 'Belwethers', which is almost completely hidden from the public view by a massive hedge and a stout door. Opposite the church is the hospital, which was founded in 1859 by a Cranleigh surgeon, was the first cottage hospital in the country and which has now overflowed the confines of the lovely sixteenth-century house in which it began.

The church itself is full of interest. It has an extremely well-kept churchyard with some handsome trees, including a magnificent cedar, and inside there has been a very tasteful restoration within the last twenty years, making good very severe damage caused by a flying bomb which landed 70 yards away in August 1944. Seven and a half years were spent in repairing the damage and yet the church was only closed for three months during that time, a tribute to the skill of the architects and the devotion of the parishioners.

One of the casualties of the bomb was the stained glass in all but three of the windows and this has been replaced with plain glass; this is particularly effective in the fine east window, outside which are attractive trees, much more pleasant for the congregation to look upon than the dreadful stained glass which disfigures so many churches. The double hammer beams of the roof are noteworthy as is the reredos of brasses which are thought to be sixteenth-century Flemish work.

The arch of the north transept suggests the twelfth century, while the chancel, side aisle and west tower are probably of the beginning of the thirteenth century. The pillar bases have 'claw' decoration and the carved head below the south transept arch is of a cat and is popularly supposed to have given Lewis Carroll the idea for the Cheshire Cat. A fifteenth-century screen in the south transept leads into a chapel with many memorials to the Waller family, one of whom was killed with the Royal Naval Division at Gallipoli in May 1915, less than a month after the troops had landed on the peninsula. The Waller chapel, as we may call it, has good pews. Of the furnishings, notice the fourteenth-century font, the sedilia, piscina, brasses and table in the chancel and the pulpit with its panels, nicely carved, from a screen which once stood in the north transept. Near the west door there is a wooden cross which once marked the grave in Flanders of an unknown soldier.

A fine, open, spacious church, then, with many lovely things in it. Visit it after passing through the village; it will do much to dispel the impression created by that shopping centre!

The last three villages of this chapter lie farther south again, in that corner where the clay is gradually defeated and subdued by the sands and gravels that take over further west. This is the corner where the suffix 'fold' holds sway—Dunsfold, Alfold and Chiddingfold.

The neighbouring parishes of Alfold and Dunsfold are described in the Victoria County History as "sequestered". What a delightful word this is! It immediately conjures up a picture of romantic charm and rustic simplicity, that pre-Raphaelite perfection unsullied by the brutal satire of Stella Gibbons. Both villages still have something of their past sequestered peace, but the fumes of incompletely combusted hydrocarbons, even here, dominate the scents of lilac in late May.

Neither village was mentioned in the Domesday record and, doubtless, no settlement had by then been carved out of the Weald forest. That came later when seams of ironstone had been located. From the end of the twelfth century the names recur, that of Burningfold more often than the present names. This was, probably, the oldest local manor, a dependency of Bramley. Its name discloses its connection with the charcoal industry that was centred here, as later in Alfold and elsewhere round the district, to serve at first the ironworks, of which, in the sixteenth century, three were listed in Dunsfold and one in Durfold. Later the glassworks of Alfold and Chiddingfold, and then the government gunpowder works at Dunsfold itself, all required considerable supplies of charcoal.

It is probable that the main outlets of the three villages of the folded lands, the result of the final squeezing of the Alpine thrust of the Miocene period, were to the south, into Sussex, down the line of the Arun that rises just to the north of Dunsfold. River navigation could be practised with small, flat craft right up to this area. It seems indeed that trees were transported from the forest here down to Littlehampton for ship-building, and one house, at least, in Dunsfold owes its great beams to a return cargo of old ship's timbers from the wrecker's yard on the coast. This is 'Yonder Lye' by the Green, so named as being the homestead farthest from the church. The old cottage that is the east end of this remarkably skilfully extended house has fire-dogs dated 1599, an iron fire-back dated 1619, the remains of its spit and bacon shelf and of a seventeenth-century children's pen beside the fire.

The main village stretches out for half a mile along the west side of the green, an expanse of rough grass that obviously needs a deal of expensive trimming. It is a village of many styles of building from the seventeenth century to today, a village of chimneys and marble doorsteps, of cottages cunningly combined and refashioned. Just round the corner from 'The Sun' is an ancient oak-tree with a 20-foot girth.

Large country houses dot the landscape. Some are ancient but quite a large number date from the seventeenth century, when one of the series of invasions of Londoners came down, like locusts, on the Surrey countryside, this time to escape the dangers of the Great Plague.

Curiously Dunsfold church lies a good half-mile to the east of the village and is set on a small hill amid a little gaggle of good seventeenth-century houses, of which one was the old rectory and one is believed to have been the inn. There is no absolute certainty as to why the village grew up so far from its church, though it seems that the church owes its existence to a holy well that can be found some hundred yards below it. The waters had healing properties, though they look remarkably unhygienic today, and they appear to have attracted a good clientele of sufferers mainly from eye complaints. As one result of the prosperity brought by this curative renown this attractive little church came into being.

It is a remarkable building since, apart from a relatively modern vestry and organ-housing, and the wooden turret and the outer door of the south porch, both probably of the late fifteenth century, the rest wholly dates from the years 1270–1290, even the porch itself and its inner door with its original, local iron-work, even the pews in the nave. Of course elements have changed; there is the usual unworthy coloured glass and the bits of encaustic tiling which are the seemingly inevitable memorial of the Victorians' ecclesiastical taste; there is some new flooring in the nave. There was some wall-painting in the nave. This was uncovered in 1903 but was covered up again. History is written into the fabric, even carved into it; earlier visitors left their initials incised into the ancient door: W x E x 1763.

The church was built in its present cruciform shape, unlike others in the county where the transepts were later additions. Each miniscule transept was a separate chapel, doubtless to serve the pilgrims. This is proved by the existence still of the piscinas there. The chancel itself has a good piscina and sedilia, the latter with shafts of Sussex marble, dug from the same nearby quarry as the cottage steps. Just west of the sedilia is a blocked priest's door, visible on the outside. A squint links the north chapel with the main altar.

The nave pews are the oldest in Britain; they were hewn for the original building. The only changes that have been made have been the widening of the seats and the filling of the spaces in the backs. The rough carved ends, like bulls' horns with balls on the points, are just as they were years ago. The font, too, is probably of about the same period.

Outside the south porch with its patterned ceiling, patterned in a red and white design some 670 years ago, in all probability, beyond the 'new' outer door whose date is attested by the little Tudor roses in the spandrels, there stands an ancient, perhaps contemporaneous, yew tree, the inmost sections of the trunk all rotted and eaten away, but the outermost rings and bark still standing, an aged senior propped up on all sides, still in leaf and 23 feet in circumference.

Few Surrey village churches are happier in their surroundings than St. Nicholas, Alfold. It is approached by a small, narrow road off the main road through the village; on the right-hand side of this narrow road is a large, beautiful sixteenth-century house now used as a solicitor's office; half facing it there is another house of

similar period and finally a big Tudor cottage part of which serves
as the church hall. Just in front of the churchyard gate is a pair
of stocks.

The church lives up to its setting. Unusually, it is nearly square
with three aisles whose breadth together is nearly equal to the
church's length, the overall effect being most powerful. The nave
and chancel follow the lines of the church built about 1100; the
massive rounded pillars of the south aisle bear witness to its Norman origin. The north aisle was well restored in 1842.

The Jacobean pulpit has the original sounding-board behind it,
hung by means of a beautifully scrolled, slender iron rod. No doubt
the odd shape of the church makes the acoustics tricky which may
account for the vicar's chair being on the congregation side of the
screen. This is not old despite its parclose doors. The chancel
contains two ancient chairs and, on the north side, a fifteenth-
century opening which may have been a squint.

The glass is not outstanding but some of the fittings certainly
are. There is an excellent seventeenth-century parish chest which
bears the names of the churchwardens of the time that it was put
in the church; the font is one of the oldest in Surrey with remarkable circular-headed arches, each with a Maltese cross, and fine
cable-moulding. The oak supports of the spire and bell turret came
from the forests which once covered this part of England; the
magnificent roof could well be fourteenth century.

Though the first recorded rector was in 1304 there was obviously
a church here long before that date. Gaps in the list of rectors in
the later fourteenth century show the impact of the plagues
while the absence of an incumbent between 1643 and 1661 reminds
us of the years during which Anglicanism ceased to be England's
official religion.

The church records begin only in 1638 but these, as is always
the case, provide a marvellous testimonial to the continuity of
country life and the all-embracing importance of the church in
the life of the community until the more civilized (?) and sophisti-
cated age in which we now live relegated the church to a subsidiary
role.

It is around this area of the '-folds' that the various rivers, the
Wey, the Arun, even the Adur, rise. Hereabouts the Wealden

M

heights rose highest. Here, too, perhaps by the interaction of clay
and sandstone, perhaps by the erosion of the rivers, the land forms
those steep, wooded waves of ground that are so typical of this
secret corner of Surrey as it links with Sussex in that no man's
land that, for so long, was only an impenetrable jungle.

Even now there is only one footpath going westwards from the
minor road that links Haslemere with Witley. This is because of
the narrow little valley, you might call it the ravine, of the Dunsfold Arun that flows north here between that road and the present
main road to Milford. That valley and others like it, cutting deep
through this district, creating bogs in winter and sheer little steeps
at all times, made travel difficult, especially from east to west.

That minor road was the only medieval, north-south road in this
part of the county. It seems, indeed, to have skirted Chiddingfold,
in spite of its medieval importance, and also Witley, and to have
gone up through Hambledon to Godalming. There must have been
a branch to Chiddingfold, for this is a village with a history.

That it was known in Roman times is proved by the discovered
remains of a small Roman villa a couple of miles to the north-
east near Pockford Farm. This was probably a farming settlement,
about the same size as, though probably more prosperous than,
the one on Ashtead Common. Later some iron was worked in the
Chiddingfold district as well as at Dunsfold, but the village only
came to the fore in the thirteenth century, when glass-making
became well established there.

For very nearly 400 years, from the thirteenth century to the
late seventeenth, it was the centre of the Surrey glass industry. All
that was essential for this was found here—the right soil, the
right sand, plentiful water. At the height of its period, the glass
industry here comprised eleven factories; there is a story, scarcely
authenticated, that since this industry was run by foreigners it was
suppressed by Elizabeth on petition from the villagers—an unlikely tale since the industry had given the village such importance
that it acquired a royal charter early in the fourteenth century
and with this the right to hold a three-day fair early in September
at the time of the patronal festival, the Nativity of the Blessed
Virgin Mary. After the glass industry declined (which, it must
be noted, did not happen until the seventeenth century, i.e. after

Elizabeth's reign) iron-works took its place until this lapsed in turn with the Industrial Revolution's discovery of new methods of smelting.

Today, Chiddingfold is one of the largest parishes in England and it contains within its wide boundaries—a perimeter, it has been suggested, of 40 miles—a remarkable number of very fine and very large houses which suggest that it must be one of the wealthiest as well as one of the largest of English parishes. Among these old houses is Killinghurst, the scene, in 1788, of a dramatic murder. The owner of this mansion, built probably at the end of the seventeenth century in Wren style, was murdered by his servant who, in some extraordinary way, evaded justice and was able to live in peaceful prosperity for the rest of his life.

Other interesting houses in the parish are Cherfolds, Roppeleghs and Crossglades. The first of these was fashioned from the farm buildings which once belonged to a large sixteenth-century mansion. This latter was used to house prisoners-of-war between 1939 and 1945 and was so badly damaged as a result that it was pulled down after the war. Cherfolds dates from 1547 and is a fascinating example of the art of conversion, for it was formerly a cowshed! In the garden is a yew tree thought to be 1,000 years old, the trunk of which has, in the passage of time, sunk deep into the soil, the intertwined branches projecting above the surface today. Roppeleghs and Crossglades are both magnificent sixteenth-century houses, beautifully kept and with lovely gardens, outbuildings and, in the case of Crossglades, a small duckpond near the entrance gate. Also in Chiddingfold parish, though only 2 miles from Haslemere, is Lythe Hill Farm, now a hotel, which is partly fourteenth century and possesses splendid cellars.

In Chiddingfold village itself, the green attracts most attention, though there are some fine old cottages near the bridge to the south. On the green is the Crown Inn, which claims to be the oldest in Surrey and dates from the fourteenth century. It has, inevitably, been very considerably altered and restored and not all the massive beams on view have always been part of the building; the furnishings include a collection of coins, mostly Tudor, kitchen equipment in the large fire-places and weapons artistically disposed around the walls, but the present authors do not approve of a telephone housed in a sedan chair! The Crown Inn attracts visitors from far afield, and its restaurant, like that of the Lythe Hill Hotel, is extremely popular.

To the east of the green are three splendid houses which may once have belonged to the 'bosses' of the glass industry (it is thought that the manual workers in that industry lived much nearer the sites of the factories). Hadmans, one of the houses to the east of the green, was once two cottages in which villagers lived until fairly recently. Chiddingfold Green, in fact, provides a very excellent example of the process which we have noted elsewhere in Surrey by which farm cottages have been transformed into exceptionally handsome houses by lavish expenditure and very skilful architects. Near to Hadmans is the fine Botley House with its glorious garden; this house has been very much altered and is difficult to date and this is also the case with Chantry House which once had the unusual name of Sandalphon. On the opposite side of the green, near to the church, are more old houses, while on the same side as the 'Crown' is Church Cottage which is less altered than most of the dwellings on the green.

The church itself contains some fragments of Chiddingfold glass in the lancet window in the west wall. This may well date from the twelfth century, the first vicar being Geoffrey de Lechlade, c. 1180. The parish included Haslemere until 1868 when the latter became a separate living. In 1559 a certain John Ellys was instituted as vicar but five days later he was committed to the Tower of London and was finally deprived in 1561. It would be interesting to know why he was arrested; he was presumably a Roman Catholic appointed by one of Mary Tudor's clergymen (the advowson was then in the hands of the prebendary of Heytesbury in Salisbury) who refused to accept the Elizabethan settlement and expressed his dissent sufficiently forcibly to merit imprisonment.

In 1642, the Puritans ejected Dr. Layfield, nephew of Laud, Archbishop of Canterbury, but he survived to be restored in 1660 when Charles II and the Anglican church alike returned to this country.

St. Mary's was restored heavily in 1869 and the porch was then rebuilt, though quite a lot of its original features remain.

Some excellent foliated barge boards in the porch, however, were lost during the restoration. Inside, the church is basically a thirteenth-century structure in the Early English style and various enlargements were made in the fifteenth century when the roof was raised to its present height. The south aisle was lengthened then and most of the former lancet windows were replaced by square-headed windows, all of which unfortunately disappeared or were supplanted during the passage of the centuries and during the restoration. The pulpit and the font are both Victorian, the former unhappily having been put in in place of a seventeenth-century carved oak pulpit. In the chancel, however, the fine chair is seventeenth-century and is said to have been given to Dr. Layfield by his archbishop-uncle, and the priest's door in the south wall is thought to be as old as the building itself. There is an interesting 'low side' window (the most westerly of the five lancet windows in the south wall); the lower part of this one had a shutter to close it when required and the purpose of the window's extension and of the shutter is unknown. The sanctuary contains two piscinas (there is another one near the east end of the church's south wall), of which the one with trefoil heading is the elder; the more ornate one next to it dates from about 1300. Notice in the chancel also the king-post which is of chestnut, not of oak, and the memorial to Charles Layfield in the south wall.

Behind the north aisle arch is the organ but plans are in hand to remove this and to restore the chantry chapel, which was once there. In the two windows at the west end is some fifteenth-century Dutch glass presented to the church in 1925. The magnificent chandeliers in the nave were presented by the ill-fated owner of Killinghurst, in 1786, and he is buried beneath them; the chandeliers in the sanctuary are even older.

Certainly the saddest thing about this fine church in the absence of Chiddingfold glass apart from the very small portion already mentioned. The Victorian restoration cannot, of course, be blamed for this, since it is most probable that the medieval glass was destroyed during the 1530s or possibly a century later during the Puritan ascendancy when so much damage was done to our cathedrals and churches.

Chiddingfold has, however, one story of damage which is quite definite and, we hope, unique. During the Second World War, Shillinglee Park, a fine eighteenth-century mansion on the outskirts of the village, was used as a billet for Canadian troops who were in residence when the war ended. This happy event they celebrated well, but not wisely, with the result that the house was burnt down, the efforts of local fire brigades to fight the blaze being hampered by the merry soldiery. Only the façade survived and a new house has been built behind this.

The village is now a sanctuary for the well-to-do. There is little agriculture and the only industry is a manufactory of walking-sticks.

Postscript

I T is impossible to travel extensively round the county as we did in 1970 without realizing the immense changes that have taken place in it during the last fifty years or indeed during an even shorter period. Places which were certainly villages at the start of this century are no longer so, even though residents of long standing may still say that they are "going into the village" to do their shopping. We have heard that this usage is still quite common in the older part of Wimbledon and can vouch from personal experience that it is the case in Leatherhead. The colour drawings with which J. S. Ogilvy illustrated his two-volume *A Pilgrimage in Surrey* (published in 1912 and 1914) show streets in, for example, Leatherhead which are quite obviously *village* streets while the fine old coaching inn which once stood at the crossroads in the centre of that village was only dismantled to make way for the present large (and ugly) shop and office building during the early thirties.

Ogilvy refers to Banstead as a village; it now has, according to the latest A.A. book, a population of over 42,000 and an Urban District Council. Epsom perhaps has not technically been a village for very many years but it has suffered appallingly since the end of the last war from development at the expense of ancient and handsome buildings, some of which were in the High Street itself. Today barely a trace remains to remind us that Charles II, Nell Gwyn and Samuel Pepys took the waters of this fashionable spa in the late seventeenth century and Epsom is just another suburban town except, perhaps, during Derby week.

As we stood one afternoon in the narrow main street of Oxted and tried to conduct a conversation against the ceaseless roar of lorries, coaches and cars; as we strove to leave the main street of Bagshot by forcing our car into the main stream of A30; as we endeavoured to inspect and photograph the delightful buildings in Blechingley's High Street and had to wait for minutes until a gap in the passing traffic permitted a quick snap; as we marvelled that the old buildings which ornament the main street of Ripley had stood up to the continuous vibration of vehicles: as we looked down upon the birth of the motorway between Loudwater and Bagshot; we could not but wonder whether Peper Harow, Shackleford, Elstead, Albury and Eashing would one day suffer the fate of Leatherhead, Banstead, Cheam and so many others.

What will help the lovely villages of the county to stave off this untimely fate? Paradoxically, some of them will be saved, as Shere has certainly been saved, by new by-passes and motorways. This could particularly apply to the line of villages along A25, notably Oxted and Blechingley. But if no such salvation is forthcoming, the villages must increasingly rely upon the loyalty and devotion of their inhabitants. Residents' Associations, Community Associations, Village Preservation Societies are happily numerous and strong; they are helped in Surrey by the local patriotism which is engendered by the annual Leith Hill Festival in which village choirs compete and then join forces to present some major choral works. Events like this, which no doubt have parallels in many other counties, do much to maintain that continuity of village life without which preservation is almost impossible. Another institution which undoubtedly helps to preserve village spirit is the cricket club. There is practically no village in Surrey which does not run at least one weekly team—Peper Harow, tiny though it is, has two sides—and the connection between the teams and one at least of the village pubs is of high social importance. Here on Saturday and Sunday evenings, city gent from London meets the man who has scarcely spent a week outside the village since his birth: cricket is the only utterly classless sport in England and resembles in this respect rugby football in Wales.

The church is no longer the unifying force that it was once

and there is seldom a lord of the manor today to exercise the benevolent paternalism which was a characteristic of Victorian England in particular. No longer is there a Lord Emsworth in every village reluctantly donning a stiff collar in order to preside over the fête in his grounds nor a Lady Constance to administer soup and moral counsel in equal doses to the villagers. The bonds forged in time of war when fire-watching duties, the Home Guard and the need to share treasured information about recipes, dress-making and other chores necessitated by rationing, together with the genuine interest shared by the villagers in the activities of those among them who were serving in the armed forces, gave the village a sense of unified purpose which was very strong and which, in such a case as Great Bookham, determined the residents to try to carry it over to the days of peace. It is a revival of this spirit—or happily, in many cases a continuance—that will ensure that the villages of England—and of Surrey—preserve their identity in the face of the inexorable-seeming march of what, all too seriously, is called progress.

Bibliography

The Victoria County History.
A Pilgrimage in Surrey. J. S. Ogilvy. Routledge. 1914.
The Penguin Guides: Surrey (compiled by) F. R. Banks. 1956.
English Architects and Craftsmen. Sitwell. Batsford.
The Weald. Wooldridge and Golding. Collins.
Collins' Guide to English Parish Churches. Ed. John Betjeman.
Britain's Structure and Scenery. Stamp. Collins.
Surrey. Eric Parker. Robert Hale.
Portrait of Surrey. Cracknell. Robert Hale.
Old West Surrey. Gertrude Jekyll. Longmans, Green. 1904.
A Picturesque Promenade Round Dorking. John Timbs. 1824.
   (Privately printed.)
Illustrated Handbook of Dorking. John Rowe. (Dorking.) 1858.
Oxford Dictionary of English Place Names, Ekwall.

Index